HANDBOOK FOR COACHING BUSINESS EXECUTIVES IN THEIR QUEST FOR TRUTH

MARIA CAMPILLO CUESY
AND ELIZABETH STONE SMITHBURG

MINDNESS
PUBLISHING

CONTENTS

INTRODUCTION

Who is this book for?

This book is for certified coaches who want new tools and a work methodology that adds value to their professional practice in the business world. Whether you have training as an ontological, co-active, NLP, or integral coach, you will find this book useful.

Our purpose is to provide coaches with tools to effectively coach business teams and our niche is transferring knowledge and life experience to create conscious leadership. It is necessary to know that we start from the understanding that you already know the basic elements of coaching and have the skills that are necessary both in the being and doing of the coach. We assume that as certified coaches, you adhere to the International Coaching Federation (ICF) core competencies:

1
SETTING THE FOUNDATION
Meeting Ethical Guidelines and Professional Standards.
Establishing the Coaching Agreement.

2
CO-CREATING THE RELATIONSHIP
Establishing Trust and Intimacy with the Client.
Coaching Presence.

3
COMMUNICATING EFFECTIVELY
Active Listening.
Powerful Questioning.
Direct Communication.

4
FACILITATING LEARNING AND RESULTS
Creating Awareness.
Designing Actions.
Planning and Goal Setting.
Managing Progress and Accountability.

Why is it so difficult to succeed as an executive coach and how we can help?

We, the authors of this book, are CTI certified coaches and trainers and have recognition as Certified Professional Coaches by the ICF. After training more than 1,000 coaches, we have been able to identify the gaps that exist between finishing a coaching training and being able to have an established practice as an executive coach. We have more than 10 years of experience coaching leaders in all types of organizations, from the new company to Fortune 100 multinationals. We have published articles and have been featured on podcasts, focused on the importance of self-awareness for one's personal growth. We are generous truth-tellers who encourage individual initiative and creativity, honor and respect "non-I" values and have an ability to adapt and adjust. As a team, we value collaboration, humility, candor, grit, and fun. If you are an executive who changed careers to coach after experiencing a good coaching process, it's first important to ask yourself how to generate the income to which you were accustomed. This book will help you create the structure for an effective coaching process for business use. If, on the other hand, you are a coach who has no corporate experience but wants to fulfill your purpose to help people experience greater fulfillment in their life and work, achieve their goals while doing what they like, then this book is also for you.

You already have your certification and have spent all your savings to prepare as a coach in what you hope will bring you fulfillment in all areas of your life. However, you are realizing that attracting and retaining customers in the corporate world is a challenge. This is because companies today not only want a coach, but also a structured process through which their leaders can obtain tangible and measurable results. After your basic training, it is normal to feel that you do not have the tools to take a corporate client through a process that will give results as well as the basis for them to use it when they do not have you.

The book is the compilation of more than 15 years' worth of experience as executive coaches and coaches' coaches. We also have experience working for a startup and large consulting company. Together, our knowledge and perspectives as an outside executive coach and an internal corporate employee complement each other. In this book, you will find 14 sessions that, in our experience, contain the necessary elements for people in the executive world to create strong foundations for their leadership, for their impact on culture and, for their structures to keep teams motivated and accountable. We have been in your shoes and through this process so what you'll read here is a collection of our skills, experience, failures, and achievements.

The use of our sessions will help you have a structure for your first executive process as well as a way to measure your customers' progress.

This book has everything you need to grow your clients' awareness and leadership skills. It will also help you know yourself as a coach, not only in doing but also in being.

INSTRUCTIONS

This book aims to simplify, clarify, and illuminate what until now has been the not-so-known world of executive coaching.

This is a framework that works for us, but use it in a way that best serves yourself and your needs. As someone who grew up playing competitive tennis, Elizabeth is always drawn to sports analogies. During the week, she would train with coaches and peers—they would guide her, telling her the best grip to use for her serve and stance for her backhand. When the weekend came, she would travel to tournaments and go out on the court by herself. She had the knowledge in her brain and muscle memory in her body, but when it came time to compete, it was up to her to improvise and use her best judgment on the court. Maybe she practiced cross-court forehands all week, but her opponent that weekend had a weak backhand so she was going to adjust and go down the line on her. The same holds true here. As coaches, we are giving you insight into what has worked for us. We hope you can use it and find it helpful; at the same time, we encourage you to mark it with your own style and use it in a way that best serves you and your business.

This is the only book on this subject that has the following qualities:

- A clear description of 14 sessions that lead the client from the beginning to the end of an executive coaching process.
- A model through which you can generate sustainable changes in your client and maintain and grow a relationship of trust and growth.
- Theory and background for each session that concisely gives you the support to be able to accompany your client during the session.
- Quotations and illustrations that help awaken the creative part of the brain.
- Exercises for the personal growth of the client and the coach.
- A format for the initial and final sessions with which you can measure if the objectives have been met.
- Tips to carry out the session with ideas for questions, tasks, and solutions to frequent problems for both the coach and the client.

How should I use this book?

This book consists of:
- Introduction: Provides the purpose of the book, who it is for, and the authors' credentials
- I, WE, IT: Where you can explore the three dimensions of leadership that the client is working through during the process that will take place in the 14 sessions
- The Model: This integrates the approach that the business coach should have when entering into a relationship with an executive client
- The 14 sessions (client handout) and coaches' guide
  to structure your executive coaching process
- The BDG framework used to measure results
- The Coaching Roadmap
- Coaches' Gym of exercises to help you improve your self-awareness and growth as an executive coach
- An FAQ about how to attract clients, report sessions, complete a process and other topics of interest
- Glossary of terminology used in the book
- Bibliography

I, WE, IT is an overarching theme in all the sessions. As we discuss in the "I, We, It" section, the session can pertain to any of the quadrants depending on your goal and the lens in which you and your client choose to see it. For instance, the session on difficult conversations could be seen through "I", that is asking your client about her and her saboteurs; "We", that is, making assumptions about the other person she plans to converse with; or "It", that is, having the tools to make it better. Our chapters cover all of these quadrants, so it is up to you and your client as to how to proceed.

As you will see in the 14 sessions, we have created a framework to structure your executive coaching process. Each topic has a session handout that your client will receive. The session contains:

- An objective, or the goal.
- Background, or theory around the topic.
- Prework, or homework for the client to complete before your session with her.
- Session, or general idea of how the session may go.
- Illustration or quote, which is meant to get your client's creative juices working.

It is important to know that the prework ranges from doing extensive exercises to asking yourself and others questions. There will be times when your client finishes her prework and when she does not:

- When the prework is completed, start the session with general questions about the prework: How was it for her to do it? What was new? What surprised her? It is a great place to start exploring limiting beliefs. If she shares something that might not serve her, ask her which part of it is useful? Be playful. Remember to always bring it back to her current role and business context—if there is no application then it is not really relevant.
- When the prework is not completed, this is an area where there are two types of coaches: 1) Coaches who will not have a session and explain to the client the importance of taking the time to have a strong foundation; or 2) coaches who are confident in holding the session without the prework. If you are the latter, we ask that you start by being curious about what prevented her from doing the prework. Come from a place of exploration instead of judgment. Then, ask her to share at least two past events where she displayed strengths and two where she was not satisfied with how she reacted. Ask her if she sees patterns or insights about these events, and, knowing what she knows now, ask her what it would look like to use these strengths.

The coaches' guides that accompany each session will help you carry out your one-hour session. The coaches' guides contain:

- Why, or why is this important?
- Theory, or background around the topic (typically more extensive than what the client receives). We recommend that you read the books or articles that are referenced in each chapter's theory so you have a solid understanding and can feel confident when coaching the session.
- Perspective, or based on our experience, the most useful perspective to hold during the session. We suggest spending 3-5 minutes before the session starts, visualizing how to come from this perspective and what might be required, as it might not be your normal range, to make it more effective.
- Prework, or the primer that your client brings into the conversation, the way they approach it might be more telling than the content itself.
- What Gets in the Way, or how to navigate potential obstacles that may emerge for both the client and the coach.
- How to Use Illustration/Quote, or a guide of questions that allow for further exploration of the illustration or quote. This is the material for the right side of the brain. Many of your executives are often left brain-oriented, so it is a great tool to start them using their more creative part to get in touch with information that otherwise would be unavailable to them.
- Wrapping Up Session, or how to finish the session. These may include ideas of potential inquiries or action items for the client

We are excited to share our learnings with you and hope this book will simplify, clarify and make attainable the world of executive coaching for you and your business.

I, WE, IT

What is BDG?

BDG ("Be-Do-Get") is the framework we use to measure and obtain results. "Be" is about the person's whole being, which will translate into what they "do" or their actions that are tethered to what they "get" or the goals that they have in mind. We use this framework so that we know all of these things are always present in a corporate coaching environment. Who do you need to be, what do you need to do, in order to get what you are seeking?

What is I, WE, IT and how does it relate to the BDG Model?

In order for a person to make long-term changes, they need to be aware of the impact that they are having on their spheres of inference. This idea is present in the work of Ken Wilber, a writer on transpersonal psychology. He divides the world into quadrants and levels of consciousness. If we want change that provides long-term value, we need to address the four quadrants of change. BDG focuses on the first three quadrants, as they are capable of change from a coach. The fourth quadrant is a place where the client may have an impact but the coach will not provide any knowledge; the coach will provide support so that the client can carry out the changes in the system after achieving changes in the other three quadrants. Below are the four quadrants:

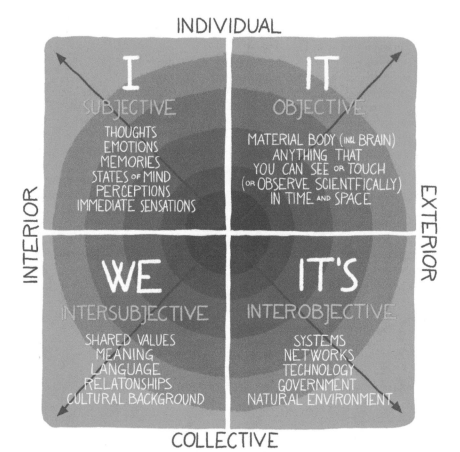

8

Often what stops a client from getting what she wants is a particular belief about the world that she sees as a fact or unchanging. BDG is a coaching process that creates an understanding with the client so that she can see how her perceptions of reality (subjective) are different from observable (objective) facts. It allows us to clearly define the area in which the coach and the client have the power to create changes and opportunities. We believe that the best way to support our clients on their path to success is by focusing on the whole person, which means working in the I, WE, and IT quadrants. By seeing that everything we do in a quadrant affects the others, our client will create awareness and sustainable changes, obtaining learning that will become actions and new ways of being.

BDG is effective because it emphasizes non-directive coaching that helps the client learn new models that encourage reflection and help her integrate them into her current reality. This will allow her to solve her own issues in her current world without needing someone else's answer or input; this leads to a profound transformation. The integral model helps us analyze certain behaviors as they relate to organizational structure, visible strategies and goals, and values and culture on an individual and group level. Each session will have to revolve around one of the quadrants; however, it is important to remember that even though you are focusing on one quadrant, all quadrants are affected and will, in turn, see change.

Values
Attitudes
Commitments & Responsibility
Beliefs
Emotional State

Share Values
Ethics & Morals
Myths & Legends
Cultural Symbols & Behaviors
Collaboration

Plans
Actions
Decisions
Performance

Our model also includes the 7 Cs, which are skills that we believe should be present in order to coach successfully in the corporate world:

- Context: This is creating a common understanding of why we are doing what we are doing and what can be expected as a result. This will enable client and coach and organization to be on the same page regarding intervention or results.
- Connection: This is the foundation for a successful coaching relationship. It is also a good barometer for whether or not the process is working.
- Co-Creation: The coaching relationship is not one-sided. It is built on what coach and client bring and what has already been defined between organization and coach.
- Curiosity: This is about coming from a place of service to the client and not from a place of "wanting to know" of the coach. It needs to be clean of assumptions and judgments.
- Courage: This is about daring to not be liked by our client when presenting them with what we see that is not working.
- Compassion: This is about knowing that when growth is happening, people are in a vulnerable position and they need us to be gentle and firm at the same time so that they have something to hold on to. We use compassion so that they feel safe while growth is happening.
- Commitment: This is vital for all stakeholders to stay committed to the relationships, the guidelines, the goals that have been set, and the actions that one commits to.

MODEL

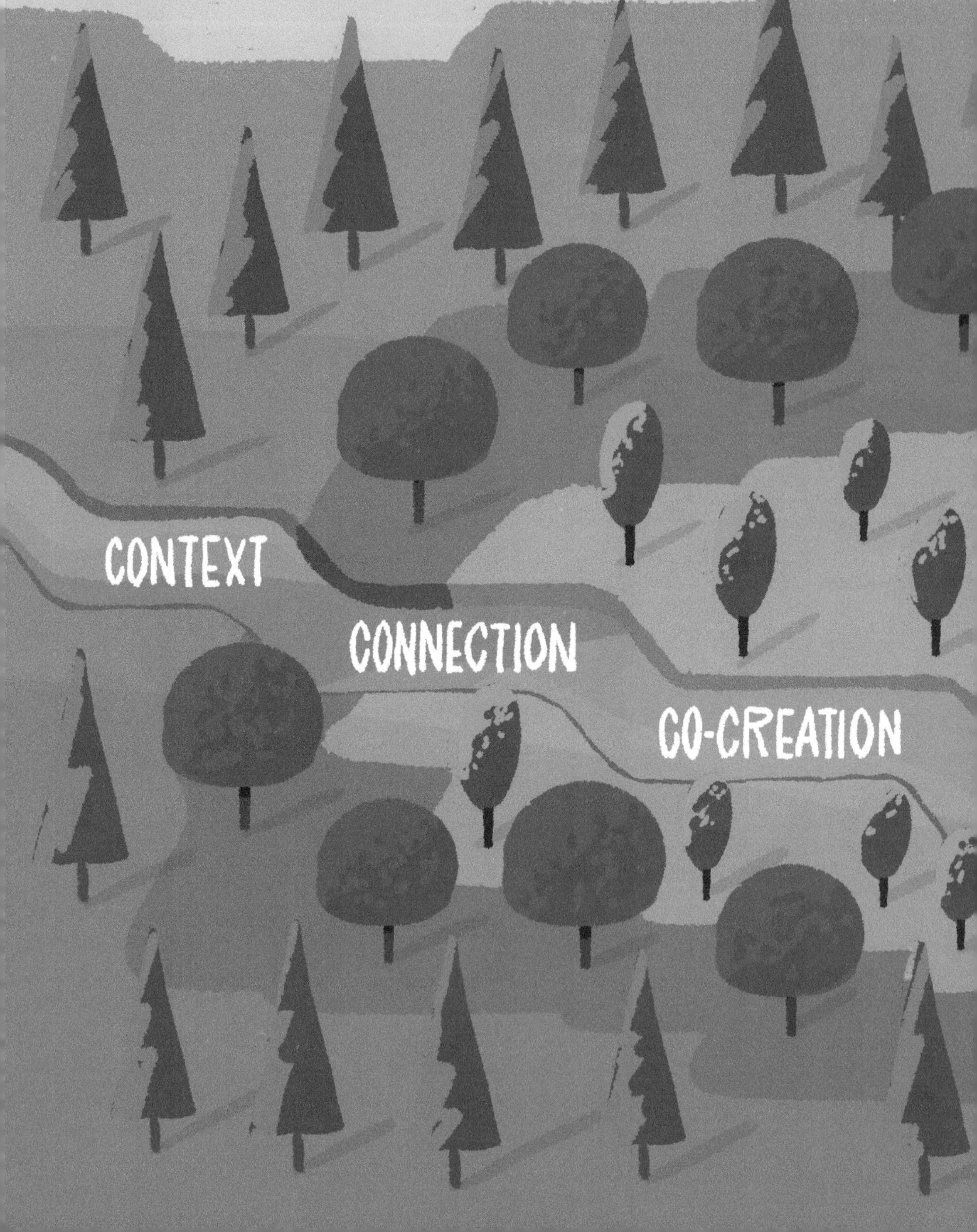

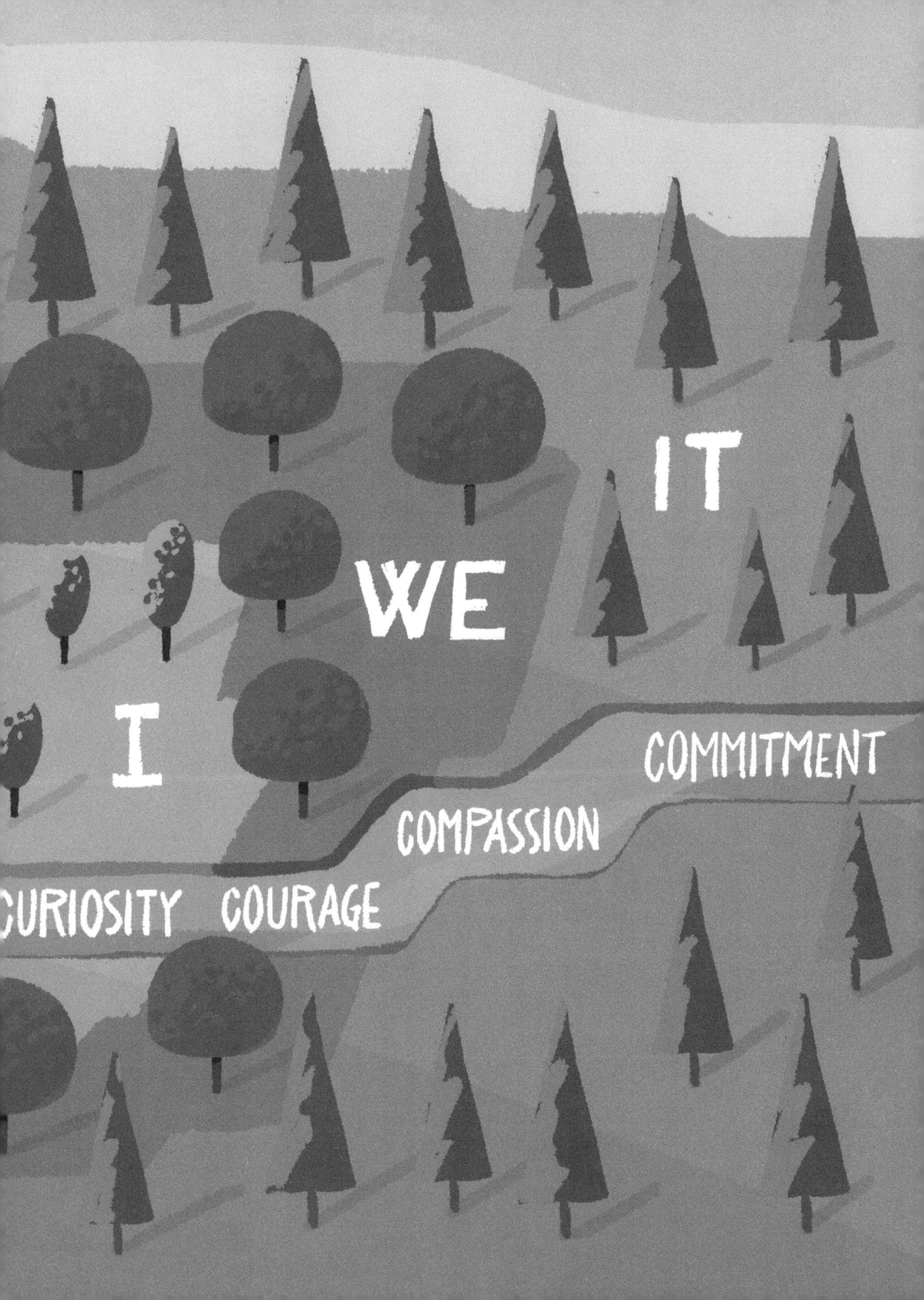
IT
WE
I
COMMITMENT
COMPASSION
CURIOSITY
COURAGE

BE WAYS OF BEING

DO OBSERVABLE BEHAVIORS

SELF

CHANGE

FROM

TO

FROM

ORGANIZATION

CHANGE

FROM

TO

FROM

Client Name

Number of Sessions

GET TANGIBLE RESULTS

SELF CHANGE

TO

FROM

TO

ORGANIZATION CHANGE

TO

FROM

TO

What is wonderful about the quadrants is that we know the interconnectedness
of them all. That is, when we know something is changing in one of the
quadrants (for example, the company was bought by another and now
the processes are going to change), we can prepare in the individual
quadrant to be able to navigate the change of a better way.

BE WAYS OF BEING

DO OBSERVABLE BEHAVIORS

SELF

FROM

TO

FROM

For those behaviors to feel natural -

What new thoughts, states of mind, or perceptions need to change?

CHANGE

FROM

If these two rows feel similar, you are on the right track.

If they don't, the organizational and self goals might interfere with each other.

ORGANIZATION

For those behaviors to feel inspiring -

What new purpose or vision is needed for greater alignment?

CHANGE

FROM

TO

FROM

Start date

End date

GET TANGIBLE RESULTS

| TO | FROM | | Start here... | TO |

SELF

If you want to get those results -

What behaviors do you need to do more or less of?

| | | TO |

CHANGE

If you want to get those results -

What behaviors do you need to do more or less of?

ORGANIZATION

| TO | FROM | | | TO |

...or here

CHANGE

THE COACHING SESSIONS & THE COACHES' GUIDE

I
we
it

① LIFE SELF-REFLECTION

To examine your past, gain insight into your present, and consciously build your future.

BACKGROUND:

While the majority of sessions are about defining the areas you would like to improve, this session is about going back to see your progress. We do this because self-reflection is not only a great tool for learning, but also a way to frame complex problems by understanding what worked and what did not. This concept is epitomized in Donald Schon's (a philosopher and professor at MIT) idea of the "reflective practitioner"— the inspiration for self and professional development fields.

The Life Self-Reflection exercise integrates the past, the present, and the future. It not only includes *what* we did but also *how* we did it—and what was happening that prevented us or supported us in our endeavor. It also helps us to take time to visualize what we want to leave behind or bring with us as we move from the present to the future.

> "The state of your life is nothing more than a reflection of the state of your mind."
>
> Wayne Dyer

PREWORK:

This exercise is simple, but not easy. Here are some guidelines to follow:

Find a quiet space, preferably at home, at the end of the day

Bring some sticky notes with you

No phone, no interruptions, only you and your life (make sure to tell the world you will be offline for at least two hours)

The exercise is divided into sections: the first is about your past accomplishments, and the second is about your dreams and goals for the future.

For the first part, you should have two different colors of sticky notes: one for personal and one for professional accomplishments. Make an inventory of all the things that you have achieved until now—the things that make you proud—from small to big.

Once you finish with the past accomplishments, take some new sticky notes and start writing down all the goals and dreams you have for the future. Be sure to spend at least 40 minutes on this exercise—anything less than that is not enough time for you to truly dig into what you most desire (this is soul-searching, not list-making).

Now divide these dreams and goals into three groups: the things you are already kind of doing; the things that you want in the short-term; and the things that you want in the long-term.

Look at your past and ask yourself: What leadership skills helped me get here? What character traits were necessary and which ones made the road bumpier? Now, look at your future and ask yourself what new skills you need to achieve this. What character traits might not be that useful for the next chapter of your life? Which ones do you want to keep?

Take a picture and send it to your coach. Take a look at your life inventory. What do you notice? What insights are you getting? What is new?

SESSION:

Together with your coach, you will review any insights and new learnings from your Life Self-Reflection exercise. Bring your answers to the session. Some additional questions to consider:

What have you learned about yourself and what do you make of all of this?

What do you want to take with you as you move from present to future? What do you want to leave behind?

Look at the illustration: What do you see?

This Life Self-Reflection exercise may have also been the start of a journey where you keep up the practice as often as it makes sense to you—it could be a daily check-in or an end-of-month (or trimester, or year—whatever works for you) evaluation. Research suggests using a journal has been one of the more successful ways of measuring changes in people and behavior.

"To state the facts frankly is not to despair the future nor indict the past.
The prudent heir takes careful inventory of his legacies and gives a faithful accounting to those whom he owes an obligation of trust."

John F. Kennedy

LIFE SELF-REFLECTION
COACHES' GUIDE

WHY?:

Life Self-Reflection is usually used as the first session with business clients; however, if you have previous engagements or simply feel that your client needs to have a bigger perspective on her achievements, do not hesitate to use it.

THEORY:

"Reflection is a generic term for those intellectual and affective activities in which individuals engage to explore their experiences, in order to lead to a new understanding and appreciation." Boud, Keough, & Walker, 1985

According to researchers, reflection is an important component in creating strong relationships between mentor and mentee (Glaze, 2001). In the client-coach relationship, the more understanding a client has of her strengths, the context in which she does or does not thrive, and her dreams and goals, the easier it will be to create a powerful relationship that will help her live a more creative and fulfilling life.

The concept of "reflective practitioner" was first introduced by Donald Schon, a philosopher and professor at MIT, who describes it as a person who is capable of using reflection both to learn and to frame complex problems by understanding what went well and what went wrong.

The Life Self-Reflection exercise integrates the past, the present, and the future. It not only includes what we did but also how we did it and what was happening that prevented us or supported us in our endeavor. It also helps us to take time to visualize what we want to leave behind or bring with us as we move from the present to the future. This process will help the client break down the self-reflection process into smaller and more manageable steps.

PERSPECTIVE:

You need to be more curious than driven in order to act or to achieve a goal. Be detached and develop a strong relationship where your client feels empowered and gains awareness.

PREWORK:

In reviewing the prework, write down keywords regarding values, strengths, limiting beliefs, and anything else that will be useful in service of your client's agenda in future sessions. This will help you to keep her accountable for her dreams and who she is at her best.

Ask your client about her experience in doing the prework: Did she like it? Was it comfortable? What were some insights? Remember that how people feel about a self-reflection exercise is part of the way they might be thinking about themselves or the world. Then, go into the Life Self-Reflection exercise:

- Start where your client was first drawn to and ask what made her start in that place. Be curious.
- What are some limiting beliefs you hear when the client speaks?
- What are the things that make her light up or that resonate about her life?
- Listen for examples where her decision was based on what was expected of her—go deeper and find if that is a choice she would take now.
- Ask which goal is most important to her. What needs to change in her to achieve it? What does she need to let go of?
- What are the most important learnings in her life so far?
- What does she want to do differently?

WHAT GETS IN THE WAY?:
CLIENT:

Little self-awareness: Some clients will go through a list of things in the past and a list of to-dos for the future. Ask simple questions that do not require her to put together insights or patterns: What did you like about that? What did you dislike? How did you get out of that difficult situation? If you ask things along the lines of "Your voice just changed—what just happened?" And she answers by saying "I don't think so" or "I didn't notice" then do not push. Know this client will need more time to get to where others might get to faster.

Overwhelming feeling about the future: When a client cannot imagine or feels overwhelmed by the future, do not try to coach her in this session. Rather, normalize and champion to her that this is exactly why she came to you. Let her know that this is something that will start solving itself and she needs to be gentle with herself.

Stuck emotion from a past event: When a client talks about a past event and she does not yet see how this is in the past and has made her who she is, it is because she is still living that moment as if it was in the present. In this case, we do not recommend spending time on this event or emotion. Like being overwhelmed about the future, not being capable of detaching from the past will make it difficult to get to a point where she can think about her future. As a coach, let her know that you will coach her a bit more about the emotion she is feeling and she should not worry about the exercise too much. Reassure her that it is good to experience this emotion and you would like to explore it further (if she is willing) and then ask her how to move forward with the exercise.

COACH:

Self-management: This is a type of session in which you start learning a lot about your client. She will display a lot of emotions, ways of thinking, and attitudes that you might find a bit contradictory. We recommend that you hold off going into full coaching mode as this could cause you to miss out on big life insights and awareness.

Getting lost in the story: Clients will bring their most poignant stories because it is usually those moments that define who we are and get embedded in our memory for years to come. Make sure to listen to the story, but do not get caught up in it and forget that the most important part of the story is how the client is relating to it in the present or what she wants to remember about it. Be gentle when interrupting, and always share your intention when doing so.

Wanting to cover all of the prework: As satisfying as it is to go through the whole prework, it might not always be possible. Make sure your need to review it all is not making the client feel rushed. If you realize you need more time for this session than the recommended hour, book a 90-minute session with her from the beginning.

HOW TO USE ILLUSTRATION / QUOTE:

Ask your client to reflect on the illustration. What does she see? What does this mean to her in reflecting on her past and thinking about her future?

On the Wayne Dyer quote: What does this mean to her? Is the state of her life nothing more than a reflection of the state of her own mind?

WRAPPING UP SESSION:

By the end of the session, make sure to have spotted your client's beliefs, behaviors, and goals. Repeat her goals back and ask if she would agree with them. Do not be afraid to ask questions that might confront her with a current limiting belief or story she needs to change. You could also start with an experiment on what behavior will work best if she really wants to start changing a belief, or simply ask what she needs to start getting a move on towards her goal and have her find a challenge.

② VALUES

To understand how your own personal values impact your everyday decisions.

BACKGROUND

In the Life Self-Reflection exercise, we explored your life in a 360-vision. During this session, you will dive deeper into understanding your personal values.

So, what are "values?" Many people think values are ethics or morals; they're not. Values are what are important to us, they are those things and ideals we value and that give us purpose. According to the Oxford English Dictionary, "value" is defined as "one's judgment about what is important in life." Thus, values are who you are in your life today, not who you would like to be or who you think you should be. They define what is most important to us and form the basis for what we will and will not do. Because values are basic assumptions, we are often not aware of our individual truths. Just as organizations have values, individuals do too.

Most people have approximately five to seven core values that identify who they are at their core. In *From Values to Action*, Harry Kraemer argues the journey to becoming a values-based leader starts with self-reflection—who are you and what's important to you? He believes in the importance of stepping back to reflect on and identify what you stand for, what your values are, and what matters most to you. Kraemer asks, "If you are not self-reflective, is it possible to know yourself? And, if you don't know yourself, how can you lead yourself? And, if you can't lead yourself, how can you lead others?" He identifies self-reflection as the first step that guides leaders to make choices aligned with their values and recounts how these principles helped him navigate some of his toughest challenges as CEO of Baxter International. Leading with values is a leadership philosophy that steps outside of measuring success by prestige, personal wealth and power. It is not about emulating the great leaders of yesterday. Instead, it is a practice of identifying what matters to you, what you stand for and what values you have in your life. With this basis, making the right decisions in life and leadership becomes easy.

PREWORK:

Think of your favorite movie, book, person, and place and answer the following questions:

What do you like about it?

. . . .

. . . .

When you are in the presence of that thing, what resonates with you?

. . . .

. . . .

Think of things that you get irritated by, dislike, or have strong feelings about, and answer the following questions:

What annoys you about them?

. . . .

. . . .

What do these things do to you?

. . . .

. . . .

Some additional questions to consider:

Describe your peak experience. What were you doing? What values were being implemented?

. . . .

. . . .

. . . .

Think of a time you were frustrated or angry. What was happening? What values were being suppressed?

. . . .

. . . .

. . . .

What things, if taken away, would make life unbearable?

. . . .

. . . .

. . . .

Share this with your coach.

"Happiness is that state of consciousness which proceeds from the achievement of one's values."

Ayn Rand

SESSION:

During this session, you will explore the things that you hold valuable in your life. You will also explore the voices that prevent you from getting them and/or from living in alignment with your values.

We will figure out your guiding principles (or what we call values). Remember that values are specific to you; for example, your values may be honesty, loyalty, and kindness or even having lunch with friends, but know that these are not the same for everyone. If it's helpful, it may be worth reviewing your Life Self-Reflection exercise to dig deep into the values present.

"It's not hard to make decisions when you know what your values are."

Roy Disney

VALUES
COACHES' GUIDE

WHY?:

As a coach, it is of vital importance that we hear what our client's values are so we can hold her to her higher self and make her aware of what is important to her and how certain situations can be resolved when we know what motivates us and makes us happy.

THEORY:

According to the Oxford English Dictionary, "value" is "one's judgment about what is important in life." Thus, values are who you are in your life today, not who you want to be or who others (or you) think you should be. They define what is most important to us and form the basis for what we will and will not do. Because values are basic assumptions, we are often not aware of our individual truths.

In *From Values to Action*, Harry Kraemer argues the journey to becoming a values-based leader starts with self-reflection—who are you and what's important to you? He believes in the importance of stepping back to reflect on and identify what you stand for, what your values are, and what matters most to you. Kraemer asks, "If you are not self-reflective, is it possible to know yourself? And, if you don't know yourself, how can you lead yourself? And, if you can't lead yourself, how can you lead others?" He identifies self-reflection as the first step that guides leaders to make choices aligned with their values and recounts how these principles helped him navigate some of his toughest challenges as CEO of Baxter International. The remaining three principles are balance, self-confidence, and genuine humility. These principles are interconnected and build upon each other. Together, the four principles can have an impact on people around the world who would like to have a few tools to get them to step up individually and make a difference; they form a solid foundation for values-based leaders to arise.

In this session, it's important for you to help your client figure out her guiding principles. Remember her values are specific to her; for example, her values may be honesty, loyalty, and kindness, but know these will not be the same for everyone. It may be worth reminding your client of her Life Self-Reflection exercise and to dig deep into the values present there.

PERSPECTIVE:

Values are worth being explored, you will bring awareness to your client on what is she values. You will help her understand her choices and her likes and dislikes. In the corporate world, you will help her see the gaps between her individual values and company values. In doing and understanding this, it will help her move into alignment (if not agreement) and make better decisions while feeling congruence with her being and doing.

PREWORK:

If the mission statement (see Chapter 3) is our client's true north, her values are the map that will get her there. Explore with a lot of curiosity and without assuming that you know what her values mean.

When you listen to a client say her family is her most important value, explore what is it in the family that she values so much and how this is important for her. What decisions in her life are in alignment with her values? What decisions are not? What does she need to do and who does she need to be in order to be more aligned with what is important?

Remember, by now you already have a lot of information on your client, from her Life Self-Reflection exercise to your designed alliance. Start to hold her accountable for things she has said she wants that are not appearing, or reflect back on those that she has said make her happy.

WHAT GETS IN THE WAY?:
CLIENT:

Competing values: Through this exercise, your client may conclude she has two competing values that cannot exist together. For instance, say her top two values are loyalty and honesty and she envisions a world where it's impossible to be totally honest and totally loyal (for example, "I have unwavering loyalty to my sister, but she also annoys me sometimes—if I am honest with her about her annoying habits, then I am being disloyal to her"). As a coach, it's important to challenge her way of thinking and reframe it in a way where both worlds can coexist.

Wanting to move too fast to action: When your client starts realizing her values, she might start seeing the gaps she wants to fill, so do not move to action too fast. Encourage her to stay in this exploratory mood.

Apathy: Your client might have been able to do very well without knowing her values and find it useless to go through this exercise. Be curious— what is it about the exercise that is not relatable? What is the value that is not being honored?

COACH:

Becoming judgmental: Your client may come in with top values like beauty and frugality. Just because your values are different than your client's does not make her values any less important. It's crucial that the coach comes from a place of openness and curiosity.

Lack of curiosity: Do not take things for granted. A value that is important to you may not carry the same meaning for your client. Make sure to go deeper and reflect back when you hear your client's voice, pace, etc. change.

Holding too tightly to a value: Hold each value as an individual entity, you might even be able to create a metaphor if the value itself is not just a word. For instance, maybe the client's value is not honesty, but rather speaking the truth like a child (for example, no filter). Listen for these subtleties.

HOW TO USE ILLUSTRATION / QUOTE:

In looking at the illustration, what do you see? What do the containers and containers' content represent for you and your life?

In reading Roy Disney's quote, what are some "not hard to make" decisions you've made in the past? What values did you honor?

WRAPPING UP SESSION:

In concluding the session, ask your client to think about when and how the saboteurs appear in her life. Journal in different quadrants how these voices change form and intention.

❸ MISSION STATEMENT

To draft your personal mission statement which will be used as a compass for your leadership model.

To remain indifferent to the challenges we face is indefensible. If the goal is noble, whether or not it is realized within our lifetime is largely irrelevant. What we must do, therefore, is to strive, and persevere, and never give up.

Dalai Lama, the 14th

BACKGROUND:

Whether it's a daily mantra or a quote for when times get tough, having a personal mission statement brings focus and purpose to your life. It's no secret that the most successful people have personal mission statements—Oprah Winfrey, Richard Branson, Steve Jobs, and Nelson Mandela, to name a few. The vision they hold for themselves goes beyond their individual interests and goals.

In Man's Search for Meaning, Viktor Frankel chronicles his experience as an Auschwitz concentration camp survivor. He argues identifying a life purpose, and imagining their future, affected the prisoners' longevity. He states: "What was really needed was a fundamental change in our attitude toward life. We had to learn ourselves and, furthermore, we had to teach the despairing men, that it did not really matter what we expected from life, but rather what life expected from us. We needed to stop asking about the meaning of life, and instead think of ourselves as those who were being questioned by life—daily and hourly. Our question must consist, not in talk and meditation, but in right action and in right conduct. Life ultimately means taking the responsibility to find the right answer to its problems and to fulfill the tasks which it constantly sets for each individual."

PREWORK:

Start thinking about your mission statement and the impact you want to have on this world in your lifetime. Some questions to start thinking about:

What is a problem you see in the world and how are you intending to fix it?

Why are you doing what you're doing? And why is that?

What would the best version of you look like?

Share this with your coach.

SESSION:

In this session, the key is exploration. What's bigger than you? Your mission statement will force you to think deeply about your life, clarify its purpose, and define what is truly important. A powerful mission statement is fully integrated into your self—its value and purpose become a part of you.

While there is no set formula to follow, William Arruda, author of *Ditch, Dare, Do: 3D Personal Branding for Executives*, suggests "the value you create + who you're creating it for + the expected outcome."

Understand that while this is a draft of your mission statement, it's constantly evolving so revisit and tweak as needed.

Some samples of CEOs mission statements:

"To be a teacher. And to be known for inspiring my students to be more than they thought they could be."

Oprah Winfrey

"To have fun in [my] journey through life and learn from [my] mistakes."

Sir Richard Branson

MISSION STATEMENT
COACHES' GUIDE

WHY?:

Leaders need to have a way to access their "true north" in a matter of seconds. A mission statement is a simple tool that encapsulates what they stand for and how they want to create impact. It is something to use when difficult decisions arise and they need to know if it will take them closer or further from the path they have set for themselves and others.

THEORY:

It's no secret that the most successful people have personal mission statements—Oprah Winfrey, Richard Branson, Steve Jobs, and Nelson Mandela to name just a few. The visions that they hold for themselves go beyond their individual interests and goals.

Richard Strozzi-Heckler, the founder of the Strozzi Institute (which uses a somatic approach to learning), asks his clients to say "I am a commitment to..." instead of "I am committed to ...". Although the difference is subtle, the implication is significant. The small change reminds us that we are the commitment, that "we strive to embody its value and contribution, and we're fully accountable for its outcome. The commitment lives inside us and moves us out from our center."

In this session, the key is exploration. What's bigger than the client? Her mission statement will force her to think deeply about her life, clarify its purpose, and define what is truly important. A powerful mission statement is fully integrated into oneself—its value and purpose become a part of the client.

PERSPECTIVE:

As a coach, you are a soundboard for your client's already present mission in life. Some of your clients will be very clear and others will not know what you are talking about when it comes to a mission statement. Remember that all of your clients have a role in this world regardless of their awareness level of what it is. Be curious and purposeful so she becomes the author of her future and responsible for her impact.

PREWORK:

During this session, you will explore your client's current perspective regarding her mission statement. Be sure to align the use and importance of having one with her before you move to craft it—this is vital in having a strong and usable statement.

- Listen for roles and effects she has had during her life. Was/is she the peacemaker, the visionary, the one who helps others? Was/is she the person who people trust, who speaks the truth, who people approach to get honest feedback or clarity?
- Pay attention to those things that resonate with her; for instance, certain social causes or people who are humble and wise. All of these qualities might be some that she might want to have at the forefront of her statement.
- Repeat back to her what you hear: "It sounds like you are the fun friend who can speak the truth when is needed. Is that true? I hear that anything you do always has a bit of philanthropy, or wanting to innovate?"
- Remember the formula of the value you create, who you are creating it for, and the expected outcome.

Below are some additional inquiries to explore:

- What is the one thing you would like to be remembered for when you die?
- What are you the commitment to?
- When making your most significant decisions, what are the fundamentals that you base them on?
- How are you different from other people doing the same things?
- Imagine the best version of your future self speaking to a large group. Something you said has had a profound impact on the audience and you are all changed in some fundamental way. What impact did your future self have on the audience? How were you and others being transformed?

WHAT GETS IN THE WAY?

CLIENT:

They did not do their prework: Do not worry too much about this, as you will have enough time in the session to dig deep. However, it's important to explore what got in the way of not doing the prework and to determine if maybe she is not interested or does not see the use of it.

She thinks it is not usable or it is silly: Explain how companies also have mission statements so that they stay true to their initial vision. It does not mean that it cannot change, but rather that they know consciously when it is time to change. In the meantime, it will make a lot of decisions somewhat simple instead of having to start from zero. For example, Ferrari's mission statement is: "To make unique sports cars that represent the finest in Italian design and craftsmanship, both on the track and on the road." If Ferrari was ever presented with an exceptional Italian design with four doors (a sedan, not a sports car), they would simply not review the blueprint or consider it for their firm. Their mission statement saves time and creates efficiency because their mission statement gives them clear guidelines of what they are and are not.

She cannot see the reason that has made her make the choices that got her to where she is: This is a good time to be vulnerable and share your own story. For example, as a young girl, Maria always wanted to be a cinematographer, and not long ago she found her acceptance speech for receiving Best Cinematographer among old boxes at her mom's house. One might think being a coach is far from that 8-year-old's dream, but in reality, Maria wanted to be a cinematographer to bring stories to people so that they could reflect on the pain and joy of others and open their own heart to their greatest adventures. When Maria decided to become a coach, it was just another way that her true purpose of creating consciousness so that people can live their best lives has taken form.

HOW TO USE ILLUSTRATION / QUOTE:

Ask your client what quote resonates more with her and what makes it more powerful? How can she use what she now knows about herself to create her own?

COACH:

Trying to understand the mission of your client: Remember, it is your client's mission statement, and what might make sense to her is not the same thing for you. Even if she has grammatical errors or words that do not make sense to you, the result you want is that which resonates with her. Also, if her purpose sounds unattainable or too big for you, it does not necessarily mean it is. Check yourself—is your mission too small?

Aiming for perfection: A mission statement is not always easy to craft, and sometimes good enough is better than getting frustrated.

Forgetting the purpose: Remember to test the mission statement with real-life situations. After she has crafted her statement, ask her for a choice that she has been unable to make or a behavior she has been trying to change. Then, ask her how her new mission statement informs her about that decision or behavior? Her mission statement will be her compass in her leadership journey, a map where she can look back and see if she is working towards what she came to the world to do or if she is far from it.

WRAPPING UP SESSION:

In concluding the session, ask your client to think about what she can do today to honor her mission statement, what everyday activity will change if she does so?

❹ EMOTIONS

To understand emotions and use them to serve us instead of being hostage to them; to own our emotions instead of being owned by them.

BACKGROUND:

Why is understanding our emotions important? Antonio R. Damasio, born in Lisbon, Portugal in 1944, head of the University of Iowa's neurology department, made a discovery. Damasio found, when making decisions, our emotions are crucial. Even when we think our decisions are logical, the point of choice is almost always based on emotion. Damasio studied people with damage to the part of their brain where emotions are generated and found they all had something in common—none of them could make decisions. While they could describe the pros and cons of each decision, they were unable to execute even the simplest decisions, like what to eat. While we might not be consciously aware of it, our emotions are an underlying variable in all aspects of our life so it's important to be cognizant of how they may or may not be serving us in personal and professional life.

In our experience, most humans have a limited vocabulary when it comes to describing their emotions. We fall back on the standards—"I feel sad, mad, scared, tired, happy," and so on. But words and nuances matter, so when thinking of our emotions, take a look at the more expansive variants:

Peaceful	Loving	Glad	Playful	Interested
calm	warm	happy	energetic	fascinated
content	affectionate	joyful	goofy	intrigued
comfortable	open	cheerful	thrilled	curious
satisfied	friendly	encouraged	exuberant	engrossed
serene	compassionate	delighted	alive	inquisitive
relaxed	grateful	excited	giddy	enthusiastic
fulfilled	kind	elated	adventurous	eager
relieved	touched	proud	mischievous	astonished
quiet	passionate	hopeful	effervescent	intense
carefree	infatuation	confident	jubilant	absorbed
centered	radiant	optimistic	invigorated	focused
refreshed	moved	merry	amused	inspired
free	tender	glorious	impish	animated
blissful	sexy	ecstatic	silly	alert
expansive	thankful	exhilarated	electrified	stimulated
mellow	appreciative	wonderful	lively	surprised

Mad	Sad	Scared	Tired	Confused
frustrated	lonely	afraid	fatigued	torn
aggravated	disappointed	nervous	indifferent	uncomfortable
disgusted	heavy	insecure	lethargic	hesitant
resentful	sorrowful	worried	hopeless	troubled
angry	unhappy	fearful	exhausted	disturbed
grouchy	despondent	helpless	withdrawn	suspicious
irritable	disheartened	vulnerable	apathetic	restless
hostile	blue	concerned	disinterested	perplexed
enraged	miserable	anxious	sleepy	uneasy
furious	dejected	terrified	dull	puzzled
exasperated	grief	shocked	bored	embarrassed
indignation	distressed	horrified	reluctant	unsteady
displeased	depressed	wary	distant	skeptical
mean	discouraged	frightened	detached	overwhelmed
bitter	melancholy	alarmed	weary	hurt
impatient	forlorn	dread	pessimistic	surprised
annoyed	brokenhearted	powerless	fidgety	dismayed

PREWORK:

Review the emotional vocabulary word bank and write a list of emotions that you have experienced over the past month or so. Look at it and choose one emotion that is difficult to look at in the list, that has some charge to it, or that simply makes you curious that it is there at all. Below are some questions to consider exploring:

What is the emotion? Fear, sadness, exhilaration?

What is it taking away from you?

When does it appear? Think about the exact moment that it appears—is it on Sunday evening or when you open a work email or right before you enter a conference meeting?

How do you know that this is what you're feeling?

What is behind it?

Share this with your coach.

"I don't want to be at the mercy of my emotions. I want to use them, to enjoy them, and to dominate them."

Oscar Wilde

"Your emotions are the slaves to your thoughts, and you are the slave to your emotions."

Elizabeth Gilbert

Part of pinpointing exactly what you are feeling is having the expansive vocabulary that will allow you to articulate precisely how you are feeling. For instance, feeling withdrawn is different than feeling tired, feeling hopeful is different than feeling exhilarated, and feeling heavy is different than feeling sad. Though seemingly small variants, the nuanced distinctions are palpable. Each word carries different energy. When we are able to pinpoint how we are feeling then we can actually do something about it.

SESSION:

In this session, the key is to explore what emotion you are being held hostage to? We will explore what is behind this emotion and how your holding of it is serving or not serving you. This awareness will help you own your emotions and learn to be cognizant of how to manage additional emotions in the future.

EMOTIONS
COACHES' GUIDE

WHY?:

If we are not aware of our emotions, we create a life where we are not truly purposeful and in charge; we come from a place of reaction and tolerance instead of creativity and acceptance.

THEORY:

In our experience, most humans have a limited vocabulary when it comes to describing their emotions. We fall back on the standards—"I feel sad, mad, scared, tired, happy," and so on. But words and nuances matter, so when thinking of our emotions, take a look at the more expansive variants included in this Session.

Part of pinpointing exactly what you are feeling is having the expansive vocabulary to allow you to articulate precisely how you are feeling. For instance, feeling withdrawn is different than feeling tired, feeling hopeful is different than feeling exhilarated, and feeling heavy is different than feeling sad. Though seemingly small variants, the nuanced distinctions are palpable. Each word carries a different energy. When we are able to pinpoint how we are feeling, then we can actually do something about it.

The exploration into these emotions and feelings dates back hundreds of years when some of our philosophers examined these concepts as they relate to human knowledge and experience. More recently, Antonio R. Damasio, born in Lisbon, Portugal in 1944, head of the University of Iowa's neurology department has aimed to show that feelings arise as the brain interprets emotions, which are solely physical signs of the body reacting to external stimuli. For instance, when we are scared of something, our emotional reaction happens unconsciously and automatically—our mouths turn dry and our hearts race. Feelings (like fear), however, only occur after our brain becomes aware of the physical changes happening.

Damasio has made a recent discovery that when making decisions, emotions are crucial. Even when we think our decisions are logical, the point of choice is almost always based on emotion. Damasio studied people with damage in the part of their brain where emotions are generated and found that they all had something in common—none of them could make decisions. While they could describe the pros and cons of each decision, they were unable to execute even the simplest decisions, like what to eat.

Why is this important? While we might not be consciously aware of it, our emotions are an underlying variable in all aspects of our life so it's important to be cognizant of how they may or may not be serving us.

PERSPECTIVE:

Emotions are neither good nor bad, they just are. When we let them be, we start discovering how to create from them versus react to them. Your job is to hold that space, their being, and mirror back to the coachee, who will do all the action work.

PREWORK:

First, ask your client what did she notice when making the list of emotions? What emotion would she like to work with during this session? Let her talk about it. Ask her what it was like to see the word bank of emotional vocabulary. How can the more descriptive vocabulary serve her in processing her emotions? Remember the objective is to feel comfortable with emotions being able to look at the situation from a clear point of view so that action is not tainted by emotions. What is the emotion trying to tell her?

WHAT GETS IN THE WAY?:
CLIENT:

Limited vocabulary when talking about emotions.
This is normal. People usually refer to five to seven
emotions, so it is your job to offer her more words
to make it easier for her to identify exactly what she
is feeling. Be sure to reference the word bank.

Strong beliefs towards certain words: Many clients
will have a tendency to stay away from certain words,
like anger, depression, or hate. This does not mean
she does not experience these emotions, but rather
she has been told or conditioned not to feel them.
Normalize them. Remind her of the safe space—if
she is feeling hate, it's OK, you will not judge her.
Also, if you sense she generally stays in the medium
specter of feelings, such as happy versus ecstatic or
angry versus enraged, try to suggest different levels of
emotion and let her choose which ones are present.

Self-judgment: Clients might say "I know I should
not be feeling this way." This is common when
people dig deep into how they feel. Let her know
there is no "should" in emotions, they just are—
so one has to work with and through them. Get
curious about the emotion—what is it about
this emotion that you are judging as bad?

COACH:

Being uncomfortable with specific emotions: Check
yourself. What emotions make you uncomfortable?
They will most likely appear in some of your sessions,
so work on your own self-management and use
the impact on you as part of the sessions. For
instance, "You said 'anger,' and I can feel it—it
even made me take a deep breath. How is it for
you to be in the presence of that much anger?"

Attachment to certain emotions. Your client
might go through a few iterations of emotions,
starting with sadness and realizing that it's more
like a disappointment. As she works through it,
make sure you are engaged but detached from
the emotions. If she says it's a disappointment,
don't be stuck on the idea that it is sadness.

HOW TO USE ILLUSTRATION / QUOTE:

Ask your client to read the quotes and to tell you
what she thinks of them—which one is most
resonant and what makes it so? Notice Oscar
Wilde's is a creative use of emotions and Elizabeth
Gilbert's is a guide into what happens to us with
emotions and how we can become victims of them.
What does she see differently? Is there a way
she would like to approach her own emotions?

WRAPPING UP SESSION:

Ask your client to honor whatever emotion she
worked on. How has it been useful? Where did it
appear that you are grateful for it? Connect with it
and ask the emotion what other ways of dealing with
a certain situation would have been more effective.

⑤ PERSONAL BRAND

To understand what makes people gravitate towards you and to create a conscious image of yourself that reflects your desired impact.

BACKGROUND:
The quest of finding one's true identity dates back to the beginning of mankind. One may argue that seeking and living one's most authentic version of self is the driver behind spirituality, self-development, meditation, and so on. In Buddhism, the "self" is not static or fixed, but rather always changing. In teaching, the Buddha described us as a collection of five changing processes—physical body, feelings, perceptions, responses, and the flow of consciousness that experiences them all. Similarly, our sense of self arises when we identify with these patterns, and the process of identification, that is, selecting patterns to call "I," "me," or "myself," is subtle and usually hidden from our awareness. We can identify with our body, feelings, or thoughts; we can identify with images, patterns, roles, and archetypes. This is what we call my own personal brand: the collection of perception, behaviors of our physical body, our feelings and the way we respond to anything that happens to us.

Our personal brand is the collection of our perceptions, behaviors, feelings, and responses to anything that happens to us. To create personal brand it's crucial to be aware of the following: present context, feelings about the current position, perception of the world/job/situation, how we want to respond to/impact it, and behavior.

"When I discover
who I am,
I will be free."

Ralph Ellison, Invisible Man

PREWORK:

Ask six people (preferably three personal and three professional ties) in your life the following questions:

How would you describe me in one sentence?

What animal best defines the way you see me?

What behaviors do you most appreciate about me?

If you could change one thing about me, what would it be?

Now, ask yourself the following questions:

Based on my thoughts, behaviors, and actions, what is a good word to describe me?

Based on my current situation, what behaviors should I exhibit more of?

Based on my current role, what stories and thoughts do I need to stop, continue, and have more of?

Share this with your coach.

SESSION:

During this session, you will explore the things that make people gravitate towards you. You will leave the session with a better understanding of your core essence and unique contributions to the world in relation to the context you are currently living. We will also explore any stories or limiting beliefs you keep telling yourself that are not serving your authentic self.

"Never forget who you are, for surely the world will not. Make it your strength. Then it can never be your weakness. Armour yourself in it, and it will never be used to hurt you."

George R.R. Martin, A Game of Thrones

"I am nothing and I am everything. Your identities make all your problems. Discover what is beyond them, the delight of the timeless, the deathless."

Anonymous Buddha Master

PERSONAL BRAND
COACHES' GUIDE

WHY:

Others see what we show them. They create their opinions by looking at what we project so we need to be intentional or we might send the wrong message of who we are and what we want to achieve.

THEORY:

Eric Greitens, the author of the book *Resilience*, believes a relationship exists between identity, behaviors, and feelings. To him, actions shape your state, so if you want to feel differently then you should act differently. What we do, and how we act, influences our feelings and our perception of self; that is, when someone does something, we create an idea of who they are. Thinking about identity this way can make it easier to let go of the one we hold so tightly. Think about it—if our every behavior constructs our thought of self and how others see us, then this identity will be constantly changing. For instance, imagine you are late for a meeting one day—people might think you are irresponsible—and, in a way, on that very day and time and in that context, you are. Instead of holding tightly to the idea that you are irresponsible, imagine letting go of the need to defend yourself, knowing that you will have another opportunity to show something different and have a different impact.

The repetition of behaviors that we know will be useful for us to achieve our goals is where we can create a personal brand. We can aim towards an inspired identity and define the behaviors that will create that identity. This may require constant tweaking and iteration as we go, making sure that we know that any identity that we can create will be transient. The concept of aiming at the desired identity while at the same time not gripping too tightly is what will help us to put our ideas forward without attaching them to our identity.

To create your own brand you need to be aware of:
- Present context
- Feelings about the current position
- Perception of the world/job/situation
- How we want to respond/impact it
- Behavior

For context, think about the following as an example. Imagine a recent college graduate interns at a fast-moving consumer goods (FMCG) company and he is unaware of his present context. He still carries his college brand—summa cum laude, overachiever, intelligent, football player, class president. When he arrives in the new context he sees his position as irrelevant, a stepping stone, and one to use so he can impress others. In his present context, he is unaware of the impact this might have on those around him, and he's seen as entitled, arrogant, complacent, a "know it all", and out of place. He reinforces this by always criticizing his tasks and wanting to do more, changing processes without asking, and going around his boss to speak with people just to network. What does this bring up for you when thinking about your own personal brand?

PERSPECTIVE:

Be courageous. Use your trusting relationship as a mirror where you reflect back the impact she has when she is conscious of her behaviors and when she is not. Be kind, not nice.

PREWORK:

Start with an inquiry about what she thinks about the quotes. Did they stir up anything in her? Listen to her response—it will help you calibrate how conscious she is of the importance of knowing herself and what qualities will make her more effective. You will be able to start recognizing themes—less hesitation, more persistence when bringing new ideas, relentlessness, warmth, and connection, for instance. When you get the themes you want to be very clear by checking with your client: Is there an archetype that suits those qualities? Maybe Cleopatra of the Pandas or the Lioness. Once you land the archetype, make sure the behaviors that she wants more of or that the role requires are present.

Now, ask questions that make it more relevant to her:

- What would being a lioness look like in practice? A response may be something like "If I have to hunt for my prey to give it to my cubs, I would try as many times as necessary and do it gracefully without losing the respect of my peers."
- What thoughts would a lioness have?
- What could be the downfall of a lioness and how would you keep yourself from going too far?
- What would you be remembered for?

In order to have a strong personal brand,

we need to ask:

- How has my context changed?
- What is the most useful way of looking at my current situation?
- What useful past behaviors do I want to bring with me?
- What behaviors do I need to leave or modify?
- What do I want other people to know me for?

Each phase in life requires us to review what qualities to bring to the front.

WHAT GETS IN THE WAY?:
CLIENT:

She didn't do her homework: What got in the way of her and her homework is already creating a brand (if not with others, at least with you). Use the opportunity to be curious. You can even say: "So, are you going to be the type of client who does not do the homework?" Make sure she knows you are saying this to prove how important it is to be aware of how our actions or inactions are perceived by others. Maybe she didn't do it because she is not the type of person who asks for that type of feedback—dig into what type of person she is. What is the cost of her not going out of her comfort zone and asking for feedback?

Feeling like she would be faking. This is common. Many of us have seen the person who is one way in front of the boss and completely different around colleagues. This person has a fractured personal brand. We want to create a whole brand—one that we are so aware of we can put some aspects into use in one scenario and then emphasize other aspects in a different context.

COACH:

Trying to get it right. Sometimes the need to land a perfect archetype takes over the session. Try to identify the overall feeling of what the client needs to focus on—feelings the brand elicits, behaviors, and the new mindset. Remember it is the client's job to resonate with their new persona, so do not give too many examples of characters—let them come up with their own.

Forgetting to test the brand. Once you feel like your client has the right brand that showcases everything she is and does in the most effective way, remember to test it. Ask her to remember a moment in a relationship at home where she felt she didn't have the impact she wanted and then have her step into her brand. Does she have any new insights? Does she need to tweak the brand to make it more effective? Do that with at least two scenarios to make sure this is the brand that would be most universal.

HOW TO USE ILLUSTRATION / QUOTE:

In reviewing the quotes, which one relates most to her? What is new for her after reading those quotes? What does she want to remember as she explores her brand?

WRAPPING UP SESSION:

To wrap up the session, ask your client to create a tagline or slogan that will define how she wants to be perceived.

6 GIVING FEEDBACK

To identify your current beliefs around giving feedback, understand why it is important, and learn how to give it.

There is no failure. Only feedback.

Robert Allen

"Make feedback normal. Not a performance review."

Ed Batista, Executive Coach and Lecturer at Stanford Graduate School of Business

BACKGROUND:

Feedback has a bad reputation, mostly because it almost never has the effect we want and because people, in general, give feedback that provokes defensiveness and does very little to improve someone's performance or behaviors which is its main purpose. Monique Valcour, Ph.D. and management professor, believes the most effective way to give feedback is to come from a coaching perspective, which deepens self-awareness and growth instead of a reprimanding perspective that ignites self-protection. In her experience, the most productive feedback conversations share the following:

An intention to help the employee grow instead of showing her what was wrong

An openness on the part of the feedback giver (for example, if you are self-protective then so the person receiving the feedback will be too)

An invitation to the employee to be part of the problem-solving process (What ideas do they have? What are they taking away from this conversation?).

When these points are present during a feedback conversation, the employee expands rather than feels diminished by management and the organization. How would your feedback conversations change if you saw your employees as brilliant and creative individuals? Additionally, research shows that feedback should:

"We all need people who will give us feedback. That's how we improve."

Bill Gates

Be specific, otherwise, you can create confusion. (For example: "Your presentation lacked visuals, next time please make sure to put fewer words and more images.")

Be about the performance, the behavior or the job, or how this impacts the company or the image of a person rather than the person. (For example: "When you show up late and the presentation is not finished it gives us the impression you do not care." Instead of: "You are mediocre.")

Allow the other person to speak her mind and listen to what is said. For example, if you ask, "What is your reaction when you hear this feedback?" and the response is, "I feel like I can't ever please you, you are always in a rush and just told me to do the presentation and making an appointment with you is always impossible," it's important to listen beyond the person. In this example, when listening beyond the person, the message is "It was not clear to me what the presentation needed to have and I was afraid to ask. I wish you were more available and occasionally you would praise me when I do things well and not focus solely on the bad."

PREWORK:

Take some time to:

Think of someone you need to give feedback to, but feel reluctant to do so.

.   .   .   .

.   .   .   .

.   .   .   .

.   .   .   .

.   .   .   .

.   .   .   .

Think of the best time someone gave you feedback and what it did for you.

.   .   .   .

.   .   .   .

.   .   .   .

.   .   .   .

.   .   .   .

.   .   .   .

Share this with your coach.

SESSION:

In order to give good feedback, we need to understand the way we feel about feedback and how we take other people's feedback. During this session, your coach will guide you through an exploration process of your possible beliefs on feedback.

GIVING FEEDBACK
COACHES' GUIDE

WHY?:
The main objective is to have the client understand her current belief around giving feedback, understand why it's important, and learn how to give feedback.

THEORY:
Monique Valcour, Ph.D. and management professor, believes the most effective way to give feedback is to come from a coaching perspective, which deepens self-awareness and growth, instead of coming from a reprimanding perspective, which ignites self-protection. In her experience, the most productive feedback conversations share the following:

- An intention to help the employee grow instead of showing her what was wrong.
- An openness on the part of the feedback giver (for example, if you are self-protective then the feedback receiver will be too)
- An invitation to the employee to be part of the problem-solving process. (What ideas do they have? What are they taking away from this conversation?)

When these points are present during a feedback conversation, the employee expands rather than feels diminished by management and the organization. Matua (2014) and Rose & Best (2005) also state that effective feedback must display certain characteristics:

- Specific: It should contain specific information rather than generalizations.
- Accurate: It should be factual and clear.
- Objective: It should be unbiased and unprejudiced.
- Timely: It should be given as soon as possible after a task is completed.
- Usable: It should relate the feedback to goals and strategies so the individual can improve performance.
- Desired by the receiver: Those who are seeking feedback will often be more motivated (than those who do not actively seek it) to improve performance.
- Checked for understanding: The individual should be clear on understanding to make sure they are getting the most out of their feedback.

Lastly, the frequency with which feedback is delivered is important. Researchers found that professionals receiving monthly feedback outperformed all other groups involved in the study. Further, "those receiving detailed monthly feedback improved performance on their key complaint measure by an impressive 46% relative to the control group" throughout the study.

PERSPECTIVE:
Hold the perspective that feedback is about growth, not judgment or criticism. It is given for the sake of the other person not our own, and feedback is about growing the other person rather than solving how her behavior affects you.

PREWORK:
Start with the example where she gives the best time someone gave her feedback. What was effective about it? What was her state of being while receiving it? What was her relationship like with the person giving her feedback? Ask her what insights and qualities would she find helpful if she applied it to the person she needs to give feedback to?

Use this information to segue into the one where she feels like she is resistant to giving feedback. What's the belief behind the idea that she can't give feedback? Explore it. What's her current perspective? Use similar things that worked for her. When is she trying to give feedback? What are the specific things that would work for giving feedback?

WHAT GETS IN THE WAY?:

CLIENT:

The power relationship or keeping the status quo of the company hierarchy. Make sure you help the client clear any assumptions she has about the company structure and its implications.

Fear, avoidance, or other blockers. With these, the client might feel that the cost of giving feedback is greater than the benefits of giving feedback. For instance, the client fired an employee after 15 years of employment. She knew she should have fired her the first year, but feared the reaction. It's important to remind the client of the bigger vision and picture here. Be curious about what's behind the avoidance.

A tendency to focus on the specifics of the individual instead of seeing them as a larger human being. For instance, your client might say something like, "Their comments in the meeting are very disruptive, which then disrupts the focus of the entire meeting. Their presence leads to inefficiency." Challenge her to see the other individuals as human beings and to see the larger picture: What value do they bring? She might say that they are a leader and people look up to them. Invite her to use that in giving feedback by saying something like, "You are a leader and people follow you, so make sure that you are using that gift you have for good." Hold her to a higher standard than she holds herself.

COACH:

Justification or collusion. This is the easy route. It can be about making the client feel that what she is doing is okay or siding with her.

Judgment or worrying too much about the consequences of feedback. Be curious about what she wants to achieve. If she wants to stop being afraid and apathetic, go into what that perspective feels like so she understands the limiting nature of it. If she wants to be assertive and confident, go into that perspective so that she feels the power that it holds.

Focusing on the topic instead of the pattern that lies behind it. As a coach, it's important to listen to what she is afraid of. For instance, if she says that no one gave feedback when she grew up in her family, then be curious and go into that limiting belief. By stopping at "It is what it is", she gives the power to the limiting belief and in turn lets it own her.

HOW TO USE ILLUSTRATION / QUOTE:

What comes up for her when she reads the quotes? How does she want to be when it comes to giving feedback?

WRAPPING UP SESSION:

In wrapping up the session, ask her how she now feels about giving feedback to the person she was reluctant to do so? What is new for her? What is different?

7 RECEIVING FEEDBACK

To create empathy towards
others by stepping into the
receiving end of feedback.

"Criticism may not be
agreeable, but it is
necessary. It fulfills
the same function as
pain in the human body.
It calls attention to
an unhealthy state of
things."

Winston Churchill

"Feedback is a gift.
Ideas are the currency
of our next success. Let
people see you value
both feedback and
ideas."

Jim Trinka and Les Wallace, authors of
A Legacy of 21st Century Leadership:
A Guide for Creating a Climate
of Leadership Throughout Your
Organization

BACKGROUND:

Although it can sometimes be
painful, feedback it is essential
for personal growth. The reason is
that humility softens the ground
for new learning and real growth
(it's no coincidence that the word
humility comes from the Latin
humus, meaning "ground"). In
fact, the most humble people
are often those most committed
to mastering their skill. They are
motivated by an internal vision of
what they hope to achieve instead
of comparing themselves to others.
However, feedback can be a tricky
topic for people to navigate, as
most people give feedback that
provokes defensiveness instead
of achieving its main purpose
of improving performance or
behaviors. This arises from a lack
of empathy and the belief that any
feedback is not only easy to listen
to but simple to put into practice.

In Learning by Doing: a Guide to
Teaching and Learning Methods,
Gibbs Graham developed a cycle
to be used in a learning situation.
Today, it is often used by the
healthcare industry but is also a
great tool to integrate feedback
in an organized manner in which
we are not clouded by emotions.
Graham's reflective cycle is a
process involving six steps:

Description
What happened?

Feelings
*What did you think
and feel about it?*

Evaluation
*What were the positives
and negatives?*

Analysis
*What sense can you make
of it? If only 2% were true,
what would that be?*

Conclusion
What else could you have done?

Action Plan
What will you do next time?

It is a cycle because the action
you take in the final stage will feed
back into the first stage, beginning
the process again. Remember,
people are not experts at giving
feedback, so we better start
learning about how can we be
better at making the best learning
out of whatever is thrown at us.

"Whatever words we utter
should be chosen with care for
people will hear them and be
influenced by them for good or
ill."

The Buddha

PREWORK:

Think about a piece of feedback that you have been unable to process and that you keep thinking about. In your mind and heart, what do you believe is causing the blockage? Now, look at the piece of feedback, and ask yourself the following questions:

What happened?

.   .   .   .

.   .   .   .

.   .   .   .

What did you think and feel about it?

.   .   .   .

.   .   .   .

.   .   .   .

What were the positives and negatives?

.   .   .   .

.   .   .   .

.   .   .   .

What sense can you make of it?
If only 2% were true, what would that be?

.   .   .   .

.   .   .   .

.   .   .   .

What else could you have done?

.   .   .   .

.   .   .   .

.   .   .   .

What will you do next time?

.   .   .   .

.   .   .   .

.   .   .   .

Share this with your coach.

SESSION:

During this session, you will explore your own reaction to feedback. This can carry some charge with it, so remember to be kind to and honest with yourself. With this, you will have a greater sense of self-awareness and empathy, allowing you to use feedback to better and grow yourself.

RECEIVING FEEDBACK
COACHES' GUIDE

WHY?:
Reflecting on how difficult it is to receive feedback is the best way to create empathy and strengthen our skills in giving feedback to others. It is also a great way to make every feedback interaction a learning experience.

THEORY:
Feedback hurts, but it is often one of the best things that can happen to us as leaders. The reason is that humility softens the ground for new learning and real growth (it's no coincidence that the word humility comes from the Latin humus, meaning "ground"). In fact, the most humble people are often those most committed to mastering their skill. They are motivated by an internal vision of what they hope to achieve instead of comparing themselves to others.

As leaders, we usually act based on good intentions so it can become difficult to hear that other people judge us based on what they see. This is what relationship expert Esther Perel calls "essentializing others and contextualizing ourselves." For example, if your client is late to a meeting, she is not disrespectful because she simply took the wrong exit and had difficulty finding parking, but when others are late, they are unprofessional and disrespectful. This is where giving feedback and receiving feedback are connected. If your client fails to connect to the whole person when giving them feedback, and she essentializes them, they are less likely to grow. The same is true for herself; if she keeps contextualizing feedback she is receiving she might fail to see the opportunities that the feedback had for her own personal growth. In *Learning by Doing: a Guide to Teaching and Learning Methods*, Gibbs Graham developed a cycle to be used in a learning situation. Today, it is often used by the healthcare industry but is also a great tool to integrate feedback in an organized manner in which we are not clouded by emotions. Graham's reflective cycle is a process involving six steps:

- Description - What happened?
- Feelings - What did you think and feel about it?
- Evaluation - What were the positives and negatives?
- Analysis - What sense can you make of it? If only 2% were true, what would that be?
- Conclusion - What else could you have done?
- Action Plan - What will you do next time?

It is a cycle because the action you take in the final stage will feed back into the first stage, beginning the process again. Remember, people are not experts at giving feedback, so we better start learning about how can we be better at making the best learning out of whatever is thrown at us.

PERSPECTIVE:
Anything that happens to us can be used for our own personal growth. Everything is feedback if we have the right mindset. This is a change of mindset from praise to growth.

PREWORK:
Ask your client about her current perspective on receiving feedback. Remember, we want her to be in a growth mindset, so be curious if you hear any negative talk around feedback. The negativity is most likely because of a bad experience and it's important that we do not make her wrong about feeling this way. Maybe you explore the piece of feedback that she has been unable to process. What does she believe is causing the blockage? Go through her answers to the questions together: what surprised her and what has she learned about this piece of feedback? Be open and receive her words. Ask questions that make her move into her ideal feedback so that she starts seeing the importance of stepping into the receiving end to help her make the best out of her feedback. For instance, ask her what she would have liked differently in regard to that feedback.

WHAT GETS IN THE WAY?:
CLIENT:

Confusing feedback with criticism. When this happens, defensiveness, avoidance, and denial will pop to the surface. As a coach, it's important to come from a place of understanding. Be curious and explore what's behind the defensiveness, avoidance or denial.

Dismissing feedback. Invalidating what "the other" has to say because "they do not know me, are not good role models, or are incompetent" is the best way to get rid of whatever piece of feedback was given to her. She may discredit the feedback because she does not approve of the source. Keep the focus on the client and remind her of what she would like to work on today. Challenge her to be in the growth mindset.

Downward spiral of unworthiness. In talking about her own feedback, it could bring up some raw emotions around a feeling of unworthiness. Remind her that in being honest with herself, she also needs to be kind to herself.

COACH:

Own limiting beliefs around receiving feedback. As a coach, you may have your own limiting beliefs around receiving feedback—maybe it's difficult for you or you see it as arrogant. Be mindful of your own ideas and belief system surrounding feedback. Do not let your own values get in the way of your client's growth; remember to hold the perspective that anything that happens to us can be used for our own personal growth.

Judgment. The client may feel somewhat exposed and particularly sensitive during this session, as the focus is around feedback. Admitting that 2% of truth is hard and could hit the core of your client's darkest vulnerability. Come from a place of non-judgment and exploration. Remind her of how courageous she is in her commitment to growth.

HOW TO USE ILLUSTRATION / QUOTE:

Ask her what she thought of the Churchill quotation and play with the body metaphor. What part of her being is being called attention to?

What metaphors come up for her in reading the Trinka and Wallace quote? If it's around gifts and currencies, dive into it and explore what's deeper. What does the gift look like? What's possible with it?

WRAPPING UP SESSION:

Over the next two weeks, ask her to ask for feedback every day about her own leadership, in the office or at home. Ask your client if she were to choose a new belief about feedback, which one would be the most helpful to her and others?

⑧ ACKNOWLEDGMENT

To learn how to create a culture of empowerment and loyalty by using acknowledgment in a natural and constructive way. To understand the value of acknowledgment: that it is a practice about growing a person, not their skills.

"We value virtue but do not discuss it. The honest bookkeeper, the faithful wife, the earnest scholar get little of our attention compared to the embezzler, the tramp, the cheat."

John Steinbeck,
Travels with Charley: In Search of America

BACKGROUND:

When was the last time you were acknowledged and what did it do for you? The etymology of "acknowledgment" is from Middle English ancnawan, which means "recognize and understand"; the current Oxford definition is "acceptance as truth or existence of something." When we acknowledge someone, we create space for them and even in the face of conflict, when we acknowledge someone, we remind ourselves that shared humanity exists between us and that we are not alone. Unlike feedback, which is about what you do, acknowledgment is about who you are.

Research suggests that one of the greatest ways to motivate someone is to acknowledge them. In 2013, Globoforce conducted a research study that showed 89% of people are more motivated by being told what they are doing right instead of what they are doing wrong. Additionally, the more qualitative data showed that acknowledgment made people happier: "Employees report that recognition has a direct impact on their happiness at work and in general. That impact is magnified with frequent recognition tied to company values." Knowing this, how can we use acknowledgment to create a culture of empowerment for our work environment?

PREWORK:

Think about a time that someone acknowledged you for who you are. For example, "You are patient, humble, self-confident, funny, honest" instead of, "You make good jokes, you wait for people". If you have not been acknowledged in the past, think about some of the qualities that someone could acknowledge you for. Sometimes it isn't in the form of words—it's a look, a pat on the back, a gift. Consider the questions:

What was the context of the acknowledgment?

What did the acknowledgment do for your relationship with that person?

How did you use this acknowledgment to further serve or motivate you?

Now, think about someone you would like to acknowledge. Choose someone who has not done good work in the past.

Share this with your coach.

> "The deepest principle in human behavior is the craving to be appreciated."
>
> William James

SESSION:

During this session, you will explore the importance of acknowledgment and how good you are at receiving it. In recounting your prework, listen and read you and your body - how you were different after the acknowledgment? Knowing this, you will explore who you are now going to acknowledge in your life.

> "But what I thought, and what I still think, and always will, is that she saw me. Nobody else has ever seen me, Jenny Gluckstein like that. Not my parents, not Julin, not even Meena. Love is one thing - recognition is something else."
>
> Peter S. Beagle, Tamsin

ACKNOWLEDGMENT
COACHES' GUIDE

WHY?:

Learning how to use acknowledgment in a natural and constructive way will create a culture of empowerment and loyalty. It's important to understand that acknowledgment is a practice about growing an individual, not their skills.

THEORY:

The etymology of "acknowledgment" is from Middle English ancnawan, which means "recognize and understand"; the current Oxford definition is "acceptance as truth or existence of something." When we acknowledge someone, we create space for them, and even in the face of conflict, when we acknowledge someone, we remind ourselves that shared humanity exists between us and that we are not alone. Unlike feedback, which is about what you do, acknowledgment is about who you are.

When was the last time you were acknowledged and what did it do for you? Research suggests that one of the greatest ways to motivate someone is to acknowledge them. In 2013, Globoforce conducted a research study that showed 89% of people are more motivated by being told what they are doing right instead of what they are doing wrong. Additionally, the more qualitative data showed that acknowledgment made people happier: "Employees report that recognition has a direct impact on their happiness at work and in general. That impact is magnified with frequent recognition tied to company values."

PERSPECTIVE:

Giving acknowledgment is a very effective way to empower people to do things they sometimes doubt are possible. As a leader, it is important to do it in a natural and authentic way so practicing these skills is very important. Focus on having this experience be a body and emotional experience instead of a mental experience. Make sure that you use the skill learned and expand it to other areas of her life.

PREWORK:

Spend at least one half of the session discovering the benefits of the acknowledgment she received:

- How did it feel?
- What was the impact on the relationship and the job at hand?
- What was important about the acknowledgment in her context? How is it that she is who she is because of it? How did it motivate or further serve her?

If the acknowledgment was not a word, then explore the gesture of acknowledgment: What was it and what did it represent?

For the second part of the prework, remember that the objective is to be able to recognize others beyond what they do for us. It is about seeing them for who they are even when they are not delivering or are not at their best. It is about reflecting back to them what you know they are capable of doing when they get in touch with their authentic qualities of being. Knowing what she now knows or acknowledges, what is she going to do? Who does she need to be to give this acknowledgment?

WHAT GETS IN THE WAY?:
CLIENT:

No previous history of being acknowledged: This typically happens when a client has a history in which doing something well is expected of her, or when she has not had anyone acknowledge her qualities instead of the job at hand. For her, the whole concept might seem ridiculous or unnecessary. She has done very well without it so why would others not be okay without it, too? The antidote to this is simply to acknowledge them, it will disarm them. For instance, "You are an honest, self-sufficient, and hardworking person." Ask them how that felt. Ask them to imagine they could have that effect on other people.

Lack of courage: Sometimes clients are afraid of giving the wrong acknowledgment or for people to feel they are not genuine. This goes away with practice; after a lifetime of not acknowledging people, it can be difficult to even know the qualities that one appreciates about them. Make her practice: Who is someone she admires, likes, respects? What about them does she like? Usually, this question elicits answers such as their courage, clarity, strength. Help her see that this is all she needs to acknowledge that person. Say, "you are strong, you are courageous."

Listening to people on a superficial level: When a client has transactional relations, it is difficult for her to see the person and she tends to focus on what the person does for her. This translates into giving acknowledgment such as "You are so good at keeping my calendar," or "I appreciate your presentation skills." Help her see the person as a person beyond their role in her life. What do you think her friends like about her? Is there a word that would best describe her character?

COACH:

Your own confidence in acknowledging: This session requires that you use acknowledgment often, especially to have your client see the impact and practice on you. If you are not very good at giving or receiving acknowledgment, it can become a bit awkward and will impact the result you want your client to have. Remind yourself of the power of acknowledgment and what it does to people. Remember that it is about the human being as a whole and not their individual traits.

Not picking up on important cues about the "being" quality of the client: It is very important that you tune into your deeper knowledge of your client. Maybe she is a very assertive executive, however, you also know she is caring and kind but she does not show this often so being able to bring it to light is very important. Remember, having her experience real acknowledgment is one of the biggest motivators in her wanting others to have the same experience.

HOW TO USE ILLUSTRATION / QUOTE:

In reading Beagle's quote, ask them to think about the last time someone truly saw them. What was it like? How did it feel to be seen? How did it serve her?

What quote resonated the most for you? What does it tell you about what you've learned about acknowledgment?

WRAPPING UP SESSION:

Challenge your client to acknowledge you, and then give her feedback. Once she knows how to acknowledge you versus what you do (individual traits), ask her to acknowledge at least 3 people a day for the next two weeks. Ask her to journal about it, recording what she learns throughout the process.

⑨ TRUST

To build trust (how to and how to be) in your relationships by exploring Horsager's eight components of trust. To create a baseline of what you need so you can trust others and see how you might be measuring up to your own standards.

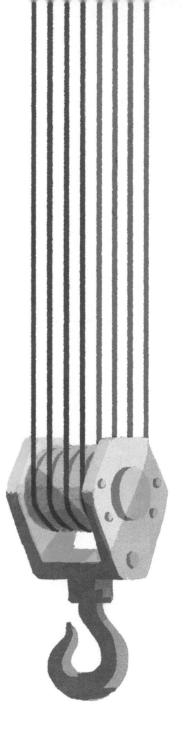

"Earn trust, earn trust, earn trust. Then you can worry about the rest."

———
Seth Godin

"The ability to establish, grow, extend, and restore trust is the key professional and personal competency of our time."

———
Stephen Covey

BACKGROUND:

Leaders must be taught both how to trust and how to be trusted. The first job of any leader is to inspire trust. Trust is confidence borne of many dimensions. David Horsager, author of *The Trust Edge: How Top Leaders Gain Faster Results, Deeper Relationships, and a Stronger Bottom Line* argues that everything of value is built on trust, as it has always been foundational to genuine success, be it relationships or financial institutions. In his studies, he found that the top organizations and leaders have a competitive advantage over others in that they are able to weather storms and maintain respect with customers; that competitive advantage is that they are the most trusted. With this, he has been able to dissect the components of what we know through that trust. His purpose was to identify the qualities that people need to see or assign to another person when they trust them. During this session, we will explore his eight pillars of trust:

CLARITY:

People trust the clear and mistrust or distrust the ambiguous.

1   2   3   4   5

COMPASSION:

People put faith in those who care beyond themselves.

1   2   3   4   5

CHARACTER:

People notice those who do what is right ahead of what is easy.

1   2   3   4   5

CONTRIBUTION:

Few things build trust quicker than actual results.

1   2   3   4   5

COMPETENCY:

People have confidence in those who stay fresh, relevant, and capable.

1   2   3   4   5

CONNECTION:

People want to follow, buy from, and be around friends—and having friends is all about building connections.

1   2   3   4   5

COMMITMENT:

People believe in those who stand through adversity.

1   2   3   4   5

CONSISTENCY:

In every area of life, it's the little things—done consistently—that make the big difference.

1   2   3   4   5

When clients are able to identify what is missing in them or others, you get to work in a target area that will result in a bigger sense of trustworthiness.

PREWORK:

Review Horsager's eight pillars of trust above and grade yourself from 1 (not enough) to 5 (more than enough) on how much you are exercising each pillar. Share this with your coach.

SESSION:

During this session, you will explore what is present in your relationships towards others and what areas need to be stronger for people to trust you more often. In looking at your prework, which of the components would you like to explore?

What is pulling you towards this pillar?

What is it like currently? Explore this.

What do you want it to be? What's it like here? What are the values present? What are you saying no to? What are you saying yes to?

Additionally or alternatively, think of someone who you currently do not trust. Explore the following questions:

What is causing this lack of trust?

What is this individual doing to you in her/his actions or inactions?

How do you want your relationship to be?

What is needed in order to have your relationship be that way?

What will you do to restore your relationship and trust them?

"A man who trusts nobody is apt to be the kind of man nobody trusts."

Harold Macmillan

TRUST
COACHES' GUIDE

WHY?:
Trust sets the foundation for strong relationships. It's important to create a baseline of what you need so that you can trust others and see how you might be measuring up to your own standards.

THEORY:
During this session, we will explore David Horsager eight pillars of trust:

- Clarity: Be clear about your mission, purpose, expectations, and daily activities.
- Compassion: Think beyond yourself, and never underestimate the power of sincerely caring about another person. People are often skeptical about whether someone really has their best interests in mind.
- Character: Do what needs to be done when it needs to be done, whether you feel like doing it or not.
- Contribution: Show outcomes.
- Competency: Keep learning new ways of doing things and stay current on ideas and trends. Arrogance and a "been there done that" attitude prevent you from growing, and they compromise others' confidence in you.
- Connection: Ask questions, listen, and above all, show gratitude.
- Commitment: Stand through adversity and do not be afraid to sacrifice yourself for the cause or for others.
- Consistency: Do the small but most important things first. The great leaders make that call and write that thank you note. Do the little things, consistently.

Researcher Brené Brown compares trust to a marble jar: "You share those hard stories and those hard things that are happening to you with friends who over time you've filled up their marble jar. They've done thing after thing after thing where you know you can trust this person." She goes on to say that we often think trust is built by grand gestures at crucial moments in our lives, but trust is typically built with simplicity and small actions; after looking at the research, Brown said "It's very clear—trust is built in very small moments." When clients are able to identify what is missing in them or others you get to work in a target area that will result in a bigger sense of trustworthiness.

PERSPECTIVE:
Trust can be built and rebuilt. We achieve this by focusing on the smaller building blocks that are missing or have been misused. When we build trust, we need to think about our trustworthiness, too—we cannot ask people to blindly trust us when we do not do the same.

PREWORK:
If the client does not understand or is not clear on one of the pillars, please reference the seven pillars above as they include what we understand by each term used to build trust. Ask her questions. What is she noticing? How can people trust her more? What needs to be said with someone she does not trust at the moment? Why is it important for her to trust others and for others to trust her? In which areas is she falling short? What is it behind her inconsistency or avoiding connection?

WHAT GETS IN THE WAY?:
CLIENT:

Cultural or familial beliefs: Trust and verify. She might say something like "people gain my trust," or "I trust, but people lose it and then it is hard to gain it back," or "I do not trust anyone." In these cases, test the beliefs by being curious, ask questions such as "What got you to adopt that stance/belief? How are you different now versus when you chose it? How is it working in the relationship/situation we are working on?"

Fear: Trusting others usually requires putting ourselves (identity, position, sometimes even our life) at risk. Be compassionate. Acknowledge that your client is being vulnerable and courageous by daring to even investigate how to get to trust other people more often. Take them little by little through the cost-benefit analysis of having other people take care of work, family, or other issues they might be holding on to because they do not trust others. Ask how real the fear is. If there are domestic abuse issues, and you sense real danger to their livelihood, do not shy away from creating the right plan to keep them safe. Remember, fear is a gift—it tells us that something is at risk and we need to simply measure the cost of keeping safe versus risking ourselves. We should never get our clients in harm's way by being naive.

Lack of self-awareness: Sometimes clients do not see that a lack of trust in a relationship is generated by both parties. If she fails to take responsibility on her part, it is most likely that the other person will not open up or trust them. Remind your client that we do not change people, but rather invite them to change by changing our ways of being and our tactic together.

COACH:

Too much too fast: Clients usually want to tackle everything at once. This is normal because they feel that without trust, either work cannot get done or the toll it takes doing things is simply unbearable. This can end up making them eager to brainstorm on what to do. The coach needs to have the strength and clarity that by just taking action without understanding their perspective and defining the way they want to approach the person could have the opposite effect. This topic could take between 1 to 3 sessions.

Making it about others instead of encouraging self-reflection: Beginner coaches may want to tackle the lack of trust as something others are responsible for, for it is easy to collude with clients when they tell us their boss stole one of their ideas, or that their husband cheated. While we do not want to blame the victim, we do want them to think about what they can do differently next time. It is also good to bring a wider view in which our client might also not be someone people can trust. Many people will get resistant to even ponder the question: where are you not trustworthy? Here, it is important to give examples: maybe in keeping up with family commitments, or sticking to a diet plan, or saying yes to people when in the end you do not follow with what they said.

The coaching relationship: A lack of trust between the client and coach can get in the way. The best thing is to not feel discouraged, rather use the lack of trust in the relationship as information: from 1 to 10, what is the level of trust you have in our relationship? What has prevented you from getting to a 10? How often do you put obstacles between you and people? What would happen if we had a 10?

HOW TO USE ILLUSTRATION / QUOTE:

Which quote resonated the most for her? What does that tell her about her perspective on trust? How is that serving her?

WRAPPING UP SESSION:

You can help your client by brainstorming some ways of being or doing that they would like to try to move their numbers in the area you explored during the session. Focus on just one, maybe two, pillars.

If you can, and the topic allows for it, create an inquiry to expand them. Is there one thing that she could change that would make her start all of her relationships above her current level of trust?

⑩ ACCOUNTABILITY

To explore your perception of accountability and the level in which you encourage others to their own accountability.

MEETS
OUTER
EXPECTATIONS

UPHOLDER

MEETS
INNER
EXPECTATIONS

RESISTS
OUTER
EXPECTATIONS

MEETS
OUTER
EXPECTATIONS

QUESTIONER

OBLIGER

MEETS
INNER
EXPECTATIONS

RESISTS
INNER
EXPECTATIONS

RESISTS
OUTER
EXPECTATIONS

REBEL

RESISTS
INNER
EXPECTATIONS

BACKGROUND:

According to the online dictionary from Merriam-Webster, "accountability" means "an obligation or willingness to accept responsibility or to account for one's actions." It's important to remember that with accountability, there are two parties at play: The person who is assigning the task and the person who is agreeing to complete the task. Accountability is not about mandating, but rather conversing; and adjusting your message depending on what motivates the other person is vital.

According to Gretchen Rubin, author of *The Four Tendencies*, we all have inner and outer expectations. Inner expectations are those that are within us (for example, a resolution for the New Year) and outer expectations are those that are outer to us (such as meeting a work deadline or answering a friend's request). From the inner and outer expectations, each individual falls into one of four categories: Upholders, Questioners, Obligers, and Rebels. Her framework explains why we act and why we do not act.

> "When one points a finger at someone else, she should remember that four of her fingers are pointing at herself."
>
> Louis Nizer

Upholders *meet both inner and outer expectations. They do not have problems sticking to their resolutions and are the employees who meet goals (without the boss checking on them).*

Questioners *meet inner expectations but resist outer expectations put upon them by others. When asked to do something, they might respond with some form of "why?"; if they receive a satisfactory answer, they may or may not follow through.*

Obligers *meet outer expectations but struggle with meeting their own expectations.*

Rebels *struggle with both inner and outer expectations. Rubin's slogan for them is: "You can't make me, and I can't either."*

Knowing our own tendency (and others') will help us set up situations that will help us achieve our own goals.

> "Accountability breeds response-ability."
>
> Stephen R. Covey

PREWORK:

Take some time to think about the following:

A current person where you feel accountability is not present. Based on what you now know about Rubin's Four Tendencies, what tendency do you think are they? What does this tell you about their relationship with accountability? How can this information serve you?

A project that did not come to completion. How were other people responsible for that? How did you contribute to that?

Share this with your coach.

SESSION:

During this session, you will explore how you are being in your current situation. You will learn about your current perspective of accountability and how you would like it to be. You will also spend some time looking at how you may have contributed to the problems.

ACCOUNTABILITY
COACHES' GUIDE

WHY?:
We do this to understand that there are inner and outer expectations. By knowing this, we are able to communicate our message depending on the person and our goals in a way that fits their style.

THEORY:
According to the online dictionary from Merriam-Webster, "accountability" means "an obligation or willingness to accept responsibility or to account for one's actions." It's important to remember that with accountability there are two parties at play: the person who is assigning the task and the person who is agreeing to complete the task. Accountability is not about mandating, but rather conversing and adjusting your message to accounts for what motivates the other person. According to Gretchen Rubin, author of The Four Tendencies, we all have inner and outer expectations. Inner expectations are those that are within us (for example, a resolution for the New Year) and outer expectations are those that are outer to us (such as meeting a work deadline or answering a friend's request). From the inner and outer expectations, each individual falls into one of four categories: Upholders, Questioners, Obligers, and Rebels. Her framework explains why we act and why we do not act.

- Upholders meet both inner and outer expectations. They do not have problems sticking to their resolutions and are the employees who meet goals (without the boss checking up on them). They are recognized as highly reliable people because they tend to meet the expectations of others; they generally do not need accountability from others. Because they so easily hold themselves accountable, they can get frustrated and impatient with those who cannot.
- Questioners meet inner expectations but resist outer expectations put upon them by others. When asked to do something, they might respond with some form of "why?"; if they receive a satisfactory answer, they may or may not follow through. With accountability, they may not need accountability for themselves, and their questioning nature can sometimes help the other person understand why they are struggling to meet an inner expectation.

- Obligers meet outer expectations but struggle with meeting their own expectations. They benefit the most from accountability; for instance, one way they can overcome their struggle is to turn their inner expectations into outer ones. Maybe they will be successful if they are accountable to someone else for something they want to do.
- Rebels struggle with both inner and outer expectations. Rubin's slogan for them is: "You can't make me, and I can't either." In terms of accountability, rebels may view this as pressure causing them to shut down or get defensive. Yet, reminding a rebel that an expectation is aligned with their personal values or their identity (such as, "I am a responsible person, so therefore I will save money every month") can reduce the likelihood of resistance.

Knowing our own tendency (and others') will help us set up situations that will help us achieve our own goals.

PERSPECTIVE:
Come from a place of understanding and make sure your client takes responsibility (such as the old adage about pointing fingers—pointing one finger at the other person means three are pointing back at you). Focus on the being.

PREWORK:
For the first part of prework, once the client has identified their tendency, share with them what you know about the tendency and explore further. For instance, if she is dealing with a rebel, ask her: What would that sound like? Let's look at them from afar—do you see this person complying with others? Do you see them achieving other goals, like finishing a marathon? Are they being a rebel with just you, or is there something you are creating or lacking that is making them a rebel?

As a coach, do not take your client for granted when they say something about someone—we trust that that is what they are seeing, but it's not all that there is.

For the second part of the prework, listen for how easy it comes for your client to blame, take responsibility, or victimize. Notice her tendencies. Make sure she realizes how she was part of the problem so that she can take responsibility and change the outcome next time.

WHAT GETS IN THE WAY?:
CLIENT:

Ego or lack of empathy. She may say something like, "I am very clear with my directions, it's their problem" or "I shouldn't be the one spending time doing this." Help her understand that something she is saying is actually unclear. What is unclear about it?

Too much pressure. Your client's tendency is something that you need to be aware of. If you are dealing with a rebel, they struggle with both inner and outer expectations and view accountability as too much pressure for them. It's important to be patient with them. Mirror it ("I notice that your obliger is coming out"). Remind them of their own personal values and how it is aligned with their goals.

Perfectionism. She might say something like, "this is all my fault" or "I should have" or "I did not" or "I knew better". Acknowledge her willingness to take responsibility and acknowledge where she did well. Then ask which ones were outside of her control? Move her into action and ask how can you go about it while actually enjoying it?

COACH:

Drive to move to action instead of exploring being. The coach might be irritated by the client's lack of accountability and see it as an opportunity to drive action forward. Here it's important to explore the being of what's behind the accountability. Be mindful of your own triggers and do not let them run the session.

Judgment. We all fit different tendencies and have different ways of being, so just because you are a certain way does not mean others are that way (or that your way is "the way"). Be open and curious about your client's tendency and know that there is no "right" way.

Your own relationship with accountability. How good are you at keeping them accountable in everything you're asking? How good are you with your own accountability? Is your client getting everything from the sessions or just what you're able to do for yourself? For instance, the coach might not like it when people are on top of her with accountability, so in turn, she is not that way with her clients. This may not be what her clients need.

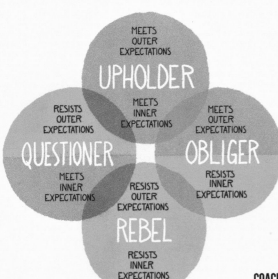

HOW TO USE ILLUSTRATION / QUOTE:

Ask your client what she thinks of when she reads the Louis Nizer quote.

WRAPPING UP SESSION:

Ask your client what would be the best way to be better at accountability? Be very specific: What is it that she is being accountable for? If it's her team, make sure she's able to identify specifically what is it about the team and what are the concrete action steps to get there.

11 DECISION-MAKING

To recognize which situations call for which type of decision-making and to enhance awareness of how decision-making affects other people.

"Our life is the sum total of all the decisions we make every day, and those decisions are determined by our priorities."

Myles Munroe

"Give people enough guidance to make the decisions you want them to make. Don't tell them what to do, but encourage them to do what is best."

Jimmy Johnson

BACKGROUND:

In our experience of listening to people make decisions, it is clear that those who make the best decisions understand the style that they use and the method in which it was taken. Consciousness on what drives a decision is the key to making sure the ground is ready to take on difficult conversations that lead to better decisions.

Style

Style is the way in which you make your decision. According to Dr. Joel Hoomans, there are six decision styles:

Impulsiveness
Leverage the first option you are given and be done with it.

Compliance
Go with the most pleasing and popular option as it pertains to those impacted.

Delegating
Push decisions off to capable and trusted others.

Avoidance/Deflection
Ignore as many decisions as possible in an effort to avoid responsibility for their impact or just prevent them from overwhelming you.

Balancing
Weigh the factors involved and then use them to render the best decision in the moment.

Prioritizing & Reflecting
Put the most energy, thought and effort into those decisions that will have the greatest impact. Maximize the time you have in which to make those decisions by consulting with others, considering the context, etc.

Method

Method is the process by which decisions are made. According to Patterson, Grenny, McMillan, and Switzler, there are four methods of decision-making:

Command

Decisions are made externally either because we do not care enough to be involved or because we fully trust the decision maker.

Consult

Decision makers invite others to influence them before making their choice. This consists of gathering ideas, evaluating options, making a choice, and informing others.

Vote

This is self-explanatory. It is best where efficiency is the highest value and you are selecting from several good choices. It only works when all team members feel that they can support either choice.

Consensus

Decisions are made after everyone honestly agrees on one decision. Only use this when: 1) the stakes are high and issues are complex, or 2) issues where everyone absolutely must support the final choice.

This session will deal specifically with decisions made within a group. While some of its elements can be transferred into individual decision-making, we are aiming to find a more creative and effective way of making decisions in an organization (such as a family, corporation, or school).

PREWORK:

Find a quiet space without any distractions.
Now, take your time to think about:

A current decision that is either not happening at all or not happening the way you thought you had agreed upon.

. . . .

. . . .

. . . .

A critical decision-making process in one of your groups (such as family, team, or organization). Now, list major recurring decisions and write how they are currently made:

Decisions in my family

. . . .

. . . .

Decisions on my team

. . . .

. . . .

Decisions in my organization

. . . .

. . . .

Share this with your coach.

SESSION:

During this session, you will get a better grasp on your current decision-making style and preferred method. You will see how comfortable you are with your own style, any limiting beliefs about other styles, and envision the style that you want to embody moving forward in your decisions. With your coach's help, you will also begin to understand how to use the decision-making process through your own experience. You will spot patterns and areas of opportunity to improve your decision-making process.

> "Only the guy who isn't rowing has time to rock the boat."

Jean-Paul Sartre

DECISION-MAKING
COACHES' GUIDE

WHY?:

The average adult makes around 35,000 choices a day (compared to a child who makes around 3,000). This number may sound astronomical, but according to researchers at Cornell University, we make 226.7 decisions each day on food alone. So, if we are making that many decisions, what is the right framework and awareness of what drives those decisions?

THEORY:

According to Dr. Joel Hoomans, there are six decision strategies:

- **Impulsiveness** – Leverage the first option you are given and be done with it.
- **Compliance** – Go with the most pleasing and popular option as it pertains to those impacted.
- **Delegating** – Push decisions off to capable and trusted others.
- **Avoidance/Deflection** – Ignore as many decisions as possible in an effort to avoid responsibility for their impact or just prevent them from overwhelming you.
- **Balancing** – Weigh the factors involved and then use them to render the best decision in the moment.
- **Prioritizing & Reflecting** – Put the most energy, thought and effort into those decisions that will have the greatest impact. Maximize the time you have in which to make those decisions by consulting with others, considering the context, etc.

We all employ a combination of several of these decision-making strategies in a situational manner. The first four are reactive strategies, and the last one is a creative strategy. They are reactive because they emphasize caution over creating results, self-protection over productive engagement, and aggression over building alignment. These self-limiting styles overemphasize the focus on gaining the approval of others, protecting yourself, and getting results through high control tactics. In prioritizing and balancing, we create the space between what is asked and what we need to make the right decision, which in our fast-paced world can make a lot of people uncomfortable.

PERSPECTIVE:

Decisions in the corporate world affect many people so help your client find the most creative starting point. Know that the right method to reach decisions will not only benefit her personally but also give others a clearer way to make better decisions based on a tangible process.

PREWORK:

For the first prework, start by asking for a bit of context. Listen to which style is your client coming from. Ask them: what style did you use for making this decision? Remind her of impulsiveness, compliance, delegation, etc. Once she has spotted its style, ask her if she is comfortable with this style? Usually, clients become familiar with a style but that does not mean they are comfortable with it; it simply means that it is the one that has worked the best. Dig deeper into how this style has impacted her life? What is the cost? Is there anything she would like to do differently? When you have landed on the behavior/mindset she wants to change, move into what method she used to make the decision. Remind her of command, consult, vote, consensus. Connect her back to the right style that she came up with before (the creative style) and then ask her: was that the right method to make that decision?

For the second prework, know that this is a self-awareness exercise. Let her give you an overall account of the big life decisions she has had and her reaction after creating her list. Spot patterns— tell her about the styles, and how some are creative and others are reactive. If you hear she has gone to impulsiveness, ask what was driving it. Fear of missing out? Impatience? What is the impact this has had on other people in her life?

WHAT GETS IN THE WAY?:
CLIENT:

Making up excuses for how they choose: The saboteur appears in a lot of explanations: "I did it that way because I had to" or "no one else wanted to make that decision." It usually sounds very either-or. When a client is not willing to ask herself how else could she have done it, it can be very frustrating for a coach. Take a step back. What is so difficult about accepting that there might have been a better way? Become curious and loving. Remind your client that the decision was indeed the best she could take at that time, and now she has more resources. This is about looking into making better decisions in the future so help them envision it.

COACH:

Being afraid of what the client might think. This is a very common mistake. People in corporate roles have gotten to where they are because of the decisions they have made. These decisions, as long as they are right, keep them where they are so clients pride themselves in that. However, it is also true that many of these decisions had huge consequences and maybe the client does not know about them or has minimized them. For example, Maria had a client who told her how proud he was of always making the best decisions. He even moved to another country when no one thought that it was wise, not even his second wife (he was now on his third wife). He then told her how he was not always well-liked but people also never complained when they got their bonuses. Next, he said that he told his only son what to study and that it was going to be the best thing for him in the long run, although he could not see it now. Maria asked him how many more people was he willing to push aside because of the way he made decisions? He replied with asking what she meant, and she said, considering his wife, colleagues, and even his kid—what if he could make decisions in such a way that he did not push people away? Would he like that being done to him? He said he never thought that was possible. He got very quiet and realized how almost every big decision in his life had dented a relationship.

HOW TO USE ILLUSTRATION / QUOTE:

Ask about the quotes—which one is most or least like her? This is a good place to start to listen to styles of making decisions.

WRAPPING UP SESSION:

Ask your client what she is getting from this session. Then ask what she wants to change about the way she makes decisions now that she knows how they can affect herself, her organization, and her relationships.

⑫ ACTION-PLANNING GUIDE

To determine the most important thing in your life for your long-run.

> "You need to be doing fewer things for more effect instead of doing more things with side effects"
>
> Gary Keller

BACKGROUND:

In his book, *The ONE Thing*, Gary Keller shows that every successful person has identified their ONE Thing. Their ONE Thing is what they want in the long-run. It is specific to them and because they have spotted it, they are able to dismiss distractions and concentrate on their ONE Thing. He argues that humans constantly live in a state of wanting more and less at the same time. We want less distractions, emails, messages, and meetings. We also want more—more productivity, more income, and more time for ourselves, our families, and our friends. The ONE Thing is about being single-minded. Once you have determined your ONE Thing, you can achieve better outcomes

in less time, change the way you work and the choices you make, and stay on track by mastering what matters most to you.

Part of the ONE Thing is also The Domino Effect. On its own, a domino does not amount to much—it's about two inches in height and 9 grams in weight, and, on its own, a domino has the ability to knock down another domino 1.5x its size. Keller goes on to ask you to imagine a long string of dominoes lined up with each one progressively 1.5x larger than the last. If you were to knock down the first two-inch domino, you would set off a chain reaction that by the 57th iteration would produce enough force to knock over

a domino stretching the distance between the earth and the moon. This two-inch domino is a force and when aligned creates something much greater than itself. The same theory rings true for achievement— creating action in small increments is the path to success.

This session will be focused on Keller's question: What is the ONE Thing you can do such that by doing it will make everything easier or unnecessary? This question puts you in a position to take control of your success list rather than a to-do list. When thinking about your ONE Thing, be sure to revisit your life self-reflection, your values, and your mission statement.

PREWORK:

Imagine you are at the end of your life and you have the feeling of ultimate success—there is nothing else left for you to do during your time here on earth. What is that ONE Thing?

Now, create a diagram of a line with the ONE Thing all the way to the right and create subdivisions of time frames to the left. Let's focus on the most immediate time frame: what needs to be done in order to move closer to your ONE Thing?

Share all of this with your coach

"What you get by achieving your goals is not as important as what you become by achieving your goals."

Michelangelo Buonarroti,
Renaissance artist

"Would you tell me, please,
which way I ought to go from here?"
"That depends a good deal on
where you want to get to," said the Cat.
"I don't much care where—" said Alice.
"Then it doesn't matter which way you go," said the Cat.
"—so long as I get somewhere,"
Alice added as an explanation.
"Oh, you're sure to do that," said the Cat,
"if you only walk long enough."

Lewis Carroll, Alice's Adventures in Wonderland

SESSION:

In this session, the key is to determine: what's your "someday" goal? Clarity on your ONE thing will help you move closer to your idea of success. It will help you stay focused on removing the excess in your life and gaining more of what you want.

You will also work with your coach to determine an action plan for the next time frame of your life.

ACTION-PLANNING GUIDE
COACHES' GUIDE

WHY?:

Goal-setting is the single best way to activate our reward system. Breaking down our big goal into a series of achievable increments will result in a greater drive and clarity, making it more likely that we will attain our long-term goal.

THEORY:

A Theory of Goal-Setting and Task Performance by Edwin A. Locke and Gary P. Latham is one of the most important books written about motivation and its link to workspace goals. In it, they describe the importance of having clear goals that are not only specific and measurable but also have the right level of challenge. They found that if the task was challenging the likelihood of completion was 90% higher than if the task was easy to do. As a coach remember if the goal is hard to achieve, the satisfaction of getting there will be bigger for your client and in return, her performance and development will grow too.

Additionally, in his book, *The ONE Thing,* Gary Keller shows that every successful person has identified their ONE Thing. Their ONE Thing is what they want in the long-run. It is specific to them and because they have spotted it, they are able to dismiss distractions and concentrate on their ONE Thing. He argues that humans constantly live in a state of wanting more and less at the same time. We want less distractions, emails, messages, and meetings. We also want more—more productivity, more income, and more time for ourselves, our families, and our friends. The ONE Thing is about being single-minded. Once you have determined your ONE Thing, you can achieve better outcomes in less time, change the way you work and the choices you make, and stay on track by mastering what matters most to you.

Part of The ONE Thing is also The Domino Effect. On its own, a domino does not amount to much—it's about two inches in height and 9 grams in weight, and, on its own, a domino has the ability to knock down another domino 1.5x its size. Keller goes on to ask you to imagine a long string of dominoes lined up with each one progressively 1.5x larger than the last.

If you were to knock down the first two-inch domino, you would set off a chain reaction that by the 57th iteration would produce enough force to knock over a domino stretching the distance between the earth and the moon. This two-inch domino is a force and when aligned creates something much greater than itself. The same theory rings true for achievement—creating action in small increments is the path to success.

Another study conducted by Dr. Gail Matthews found that more than 70% of the study participants who sent weekly updates to a friend reported successful goal achievement compared to 35% who kept their goals to themselves (and did not write them down).

Setting big goals that motivate your client is important. However, it is more important for her to see the timeline of achievable but challenging goals along the way. While it may sound corny to have her tell others about her goal, Matthews's research does suggest she not keep it to herself.

PERSPECTIVE:

Different goals require different behaviors. It is imperative that your client becomes aware that setting goals will mean defining new ways of being.

PREWORK:

The client usually comes in with a vague idea of how her timeline looks. Give her enough time to explain her big goal and listen for resonance when you hear it. Remember to also bring out dissonance when she feels overwhelmed about the goal or the lack of clarity. Work from the end goal back in time, dividing in half each time. For instance, if the end goal is 20 years, ask her what would she need to be doing in year 10 for that 20-year goal to be true, then ask what about in the next five, in the next two-and-a-half, and so on. Pause and explore the behaviors that go with achieving those goals. If in 20 years she wants to have a second home, then ask her what made that possible? Did she become more frugal with spending? Did she become more assertive and ask for the raise she deserved?

WHAT GETS IN THE WAY?:
CLIENT:

Feeling overwhelmed: Breaking down the goal into smaller chunks can feel overwhelming like there are too many things to be done. Make sure to pause and ask the client if she feels like she can achieve these milestones or if she needs to get help or move her final goal. Use your intuition—sometimes clients get so excited that they overcommit and do not achieve their first milestones, which leads to a motivation loss which can be hard to regain.

Not doing homework: Be curious. What was it about the homework that they are avoiding?

COACH:

Keeping it pacey: This session will require intruding in order to get from the big picture to the concrete behavior and action. Do not be afraid of leading the session too much and be mindful that in each stage, the client needs to figure out what concrete actions to take and what habits to modify. For instance, Maria had a client who wanted to learn a new language in order to move to another assignment within her company. She wanted to be able to understand enough to follow meetings in less than a year. First, Maria and her client needed to make sure that the client's defined timeline was less than a year—could be 11 or two months. She decided 12 months was actually going to be realistic for her since she already spoke two other languages that were similar to the one she wanted to learn. She started with 12 months, then made sure she was clear on what "understanding enough" means. For her, it is enough so that she knew the topic and could read simple PowerPoint presentations related to her expertise. This was crucial, as she realized she did not want to spend time learning common everyday phrases but rather making sure she knew the most common words of her trade in the foreign language. In 12 months, she wanted to know 30 verbs and 200 trade-specific words.

HOW TO USE ILLUSTRATION / QUOTE:

Ask the client which quote was the most dissonant and/or resonant for her? Explore them.

WRAPPING UP SESSION:

Ask your client the following questions to test if the goals you have set will create the motivation:
- Does your goal look closer?
- Does your goal feel easier but still challenging to accomplish?
- Do you have clear steps to work towards your goal starting today?
- Have you chosen how do you want to be when doing all of these tasks?

13 RANK AND PRIVILEGE

To become fully conscious of the roles of both privilege and rank. This awareness will allow for less abuse and to become more efficient when influencing others.

BACKGROUND:

With rank and privilege comes power. With power comes responsibility. Thus, when used without awareness, both rank and privilege can inflict enormous harm upon others. Bringing awareness into our own rank and privilege will make us more conscious leaders and allow us to use our power wisely to help others. So, what are privilege and rank?

Privilege is a right given only to some, and not all. Some privileges are granted based on merit, like gaining entry to a school's alumni body. Others are based on unearned factors such as ethnicity or gender. Rank is an accumulation of power and privilege that is situational and changes over time.

According to Arnold Mindell, an American author, therapist, and teacher, there are three types of rank:

> Social rank is almost always unearned based on nationality, family, gender, ethnicity.
>
> Situational rank is situational and individual specific. What might provide a rank in a certain space, like being a priest in your church, might not grant rank in another space where your title does not grant you power or privilege.
>
> Psychological rank is gained by the challenges that we overcome over a lifetime of experiences. A person who has high psychological rank will be more likely to become a leader in an organization because it will show in the way they speak, act and make decisions.

We all do things unconsciously that will bring out the differences in rank around us. Thus, it is important to become conscious of them so that we can more easily see when the context is needed instead of behaving as if everyone around us had the same privileges. One extreme but useful example of someone unaware of her privilege was Marie Antoinette who (legend has it), in the middle of the French Revolution, was told of the people who had no bread to eat and she replied: "Let them eat cake!"

Let us now explore our own rank and privileges.

PREWORK:

Take some time to answer the following questions:

What ethnic group do you belong to? Is this the dominant ethnic group?

What is your educational history, profession, sex, sexual orientation, religion, economic class, relationship status, age, physical condition? What advantages do you have because of these?

What advantages, such as access to housing, employment, services, and legal privileges might you suffer as a result of your identity? Can you access social power? Are you the target of subtle prejudice because of identity? Do you feel you belong to the majority? Can you exercise intellectual, social or financial power?

What privileges come with being able-bodied and well or young? What can you do that others perhaps cannot do or cannot do as easily?

Was your childhood happy, safe and well-provisioned? Are you optimistic, free from anxiety and supported socially?

Share your answers with your coach.

SESSION:

There is nothing wrong with either rank or privilege. Trouble arises when these advantages are held and used without awareness. Your coach will help you explore your feeling surrounding this topic and will help you come up with a strategy to use rank and privilege wisely among your peers.

"Rank does not confer privilege or give power. It imposes responsibility."

Peter Drucker

RANK AND PRIVILEGE
COACHES' GUIDE

WHY?:
Unawareness of our own rank and privilege can result in uncomfortable interactions at best and serious consequences at worst. Bringing awareness into how we are perceived and how to use our power will make us better leaders.

THEORY:
Privilege is a right given only to some, and not all. Some privileges are granted based on merit, like gaining entry to a school's alumni body. Others are based on unearned factors such as ethnicity or gender. Rank is an accumulation of power and privilege that is situational and changes over time.

According to Arnold Mindell, an American author, therapist, and teacher, there are 3 types of rank:

- Social rank is almost always unearned based on nationality, family, gender, ethnicity.
- Situational rank is situational and individual specific. What might provide rank in a certain space, like being a priest in your church, might not grant rank in another space where your title does not grant you power or privilege.
- Psychological rank is gained by the challenges that we overcome over a lifetime of experiences. A person who has high psychological rank will be more likely to become a leader in an organization because it will show in the way they speak, act and make decisions.

In organizations, all of these ranks come into play, and typically, people with lower rank are aware of what those on top have access to which they do not. For instance, a company owner may have a designated parking space, or ask personal assistants to do personal errands; these are privileges that people below him do not have and are very apparent.

We all do things unconsciously that will bring out the differences in rank around us. Thus, it is important to become conscious of them so that we can more easily see when the context is needed instead of behaving as if everyone around us has the same privileges.

One extreme but useful example of someone unaware of her privilege was Marie Antoinette who (legend has it), in the middle of the French Revolution, was told of the starving people who had no bread to eat and she replied: "Let them eat cake!"

So, let us do some introspection and look at our own rank and privileges.

PERSPECTIVE:
In this coaching relationship, just like in any other relationship, rank and privilege are present. It is a mirror of what the world at large looks like and as a coach you must use it for the benefit of the client.

PREWORK:
If guilt appears when your client realizes her position in relation to others, make sure to normalize it and empower her. There is nothing she can do to change where she was born in this society, but depending on where that is she has the power to use it wisely and help others.
First, ask your client to introduce herself from a rank and privileged perspective. Do this by role modeling yourself: "I was born in an X class family, in X country, I have X number of degrees, my skin color is X, and I have the following religious or sports affiliations," and so on. What is your context? For instance, being Irish American is different than being African American. If you or your parents are immigrants, what part does that play? This is a part of your history, so you can choose to make it part of your identity or not. How do you make it part of your identity? How do these questions apply to your client?
Ask how it feels to introduce herself like that? What was it like to hear you introduce yourself that way? What insights is she gaining from his experience?
Ask what is the unintended impact she might be having on others because of her rank and privilege? Explore when it is that she has used it consciously. As the topic for this session, you can ask her to explore a team dynamic that is not currently working and see how her privilege and rank are impacting it.

WHAT GETS IN THE WAY?:
CLIENT:

Shame: This session is not about making anyone feel ashamed of where they are in society—some of the ranks people attain are a result of hard work and years of studying, volunteering, being exemplary citizens. Others—like age, gender, ethnicity—are simply luck and we need to be responsible for not misusing it. Help your client feel proud of being who she is, who (for example) uses her privilege to give voice to minorities, who shares knowledge that was tacit to her because of the place she was raised or the people that she has gotten to meet because of her upbringing. Help her see that because of someone else's rank what she might see as a very simple question (perhaps, "Could you bring me a coffee on your way to my office?"), could be misinterpreted. Setting the context in this situation is important and being aware of the possible effect is very useful.

Too much self-awareness: Suddenly realizing so much about yourself can make one decide not to share, and that is also not the point for your client. Learn how to do it tactfully and responsibly. When we are able to tell stories we become three-dimensional. We want to be seen.

Justification: "I earned this and don't tell me that this is just a given." Help your client strip the layers back and normalize it. Bring a lot of acknowledgment.

Lack of congruency: Mentally doing something, but actually doing something else. Are we willing to do the hard thing? For instance, there's a tendency to want to sell material possessions and go help refugees in Rwanda, but the idea here is how can you level the playing field in your own environment—that is, how to treat your cleaning lady, help minorities, and so on. Help the client be congruent to the point that they feel that it's doable and they aren't going to feel unsafe.

COACH:

Lack of awareness of your own rank and privilege: This is a big roadblock in this session. It is important that you are vulnerable and share examples where you have been unaware of your impact and that you do it with grace. Rank sometimes shows up when we are not at our best, usually when we lost our patience or we can't seem to get people to agree with us. The most typical sentences attached to rank start with: "I have been in the company for X amount of years," or "I have the support of this and that person," or "Who is the one who has the title to make the decision..."

HOW TO USE ILLUSTRATION / QUOTE:

In looking at the illustration, what does your client see? What does this bring up for her regarding her privilege and rank?

In reading Peter Drucker's quote, what are some of her responsibilities? How is she going to remind herself of her own power?

WRAPPING UP SESSION:

In concluding the session, ask your client to think about the following: What value do you see in your own story? How are you going to remind yourself of your own power? And, how can you use your power to help others?

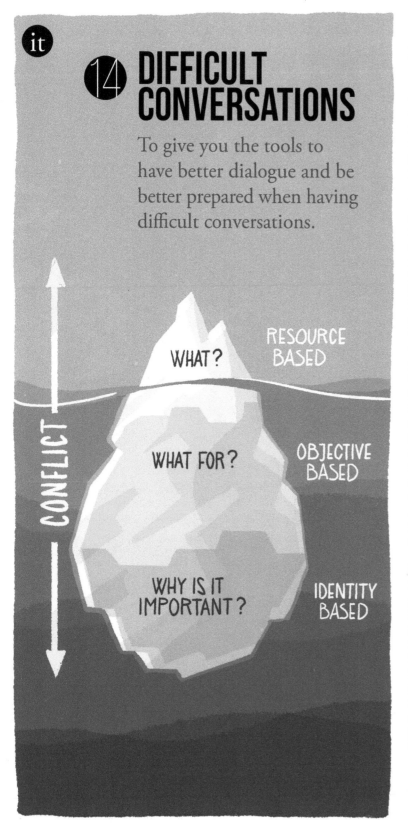

14 DIFFICULT CONVERSATIONS

To give you the tools to have better dialogue and be better prepared when having difficult conversations.

WHAT? — RESOURCE BASED

WHAT FOR? — OBJECTIVE BASED

WHY IS IT IMPORTANT? — IDENTITY BASED

CONFLICT

BACKGROUND:

In order to have the tools to have better dialogue, it is first important to understand what truly drives conflict. Jay Rothman, professor of Conflict Management at Bar-Ilan University, imagines conflict as something like the iceberg model below.

This shows how a conflict over resources (who gets what) is usually the most visible aspect of any disagreement. Yet, underneath the argument is a layer of conflicting objectives. One layer deeper are the fundamental issues around identities and personal values. It is important to distinguish the layers to understand what is happening with you and the other individual so that you are able to discuss the real issues. In order to do this, empathy needs to be present. So, what is empathy and why is it important? The term "empathy" was first introduced by psychologist Edward B. Titchener in 1909 and translates as German term *einfühlung*, meaning "feeling into." Empathy involves the ability to put yourself in someone else's position and feel what they must be feeling.

With difficult conversations, the idea is to have empathy present—to have an open heart that allows for greater connection and better dialogue. Let's increase the frequency with which we function from a place of "help me understand where you are coming from." In order to do this, we first need to understand where we are coming from and be clear in purpose, attitude, assumptions, emotions, and solutions.

PREWORK:

Take some time to think of a difficult conversation you have been putting off. What's your current perspective of it? What's your fear? What limiting beliefs are present? What are you tolerating by not having the conversation? What could be possible with this conversation? Now, imagine you are going to have the conversation with this individual, and ask yourself the following questions

What do I blame the other side for in this conflict?

. . . .

. . . .

. . . .

Why is this issue so important to me
(think of the iceberg model)?

. . . .

. . . .

. . . .

What did I do to contribute to the conflict (be kind but honest)?

. . . .

. . . .

And then, repeat the questions from the other side's perspective:

What might the other side blame me for in this disagreement?

. . . .

. . . .

. . . .

Why is this issue so important to them?

. . . .

. . . .

. . . .

What have they contributed to the conflict?

. . . .

. . . .

. . . .

Share this with your coach. Together, you will clarify your purpose, understand attitudes, unearth assumptions, work through emotions, and be empathetic and ready to co-create solutions.

"Learning that you can't control the other person's reaction, and that it can be destructive to try, can be incredibly liberating. It not only gives the other person the space to react however they need to, but also takes a huge amount of pressure off you. You will learn things about yourself based on their reaction, but if you are prepared to learn, you'll feel free from the desperate need for their reaction to go one certain way."

Douglas Stone,
Difficult Conversations:
How to Discuss What Matters Most

SESSION:

During this session, you will work with your coach to explore your current perspective and move to a more productive one. You will start to see the other person as a human being rather than a tool or object. Your coach may also roleplay the conversation with you.

DIFFICULT CONVERSATIONS
COACHES' GUIDE

WHY?:

We all have felt chills when someone tells us "we need to talk," or we have also felt reluctant to approach conversations that we know are not going to be easy. Difficult conversations are tough, but also crucial, which is why it is important to have the tools that will help guide you through tough and uncomfortable conversations.

THEORY:

According to Daniel Goleman, science journalist and author of *Emotional Intelligence*, there are three types of empathy:

- Cognitive Empathy: This is "try to walk a mile in someone else's shoes"—it is the awareness and understanding of someone else's perspective which is essential for good communication and connection.
- Social Empathy: This is "sensing in yourself what another person might be feeling". For him, this is all about rapport and you can only have rapport if you "pay full attention to the other human being."
- Empathetic Concern: This is not just about feeling someone else's distress, but also wanting to help them. He goes on to say "it draws on a third part of the brain called 'ancient mammalian system for parenting'. It's like a parent's love for a child. If you have that love for someone, you're going to be there for them."

According to him, having all three is the key to having better and more successful relationships. As imperfect human beings subject to a certain genetic makeup and social conditioning, sometimes we are empathetic and sometimes we are not. Empathy leads to helping behavior which strengthens social relationships. When empathy is present so is an ability and willingness to understand another person's story and perspective. There is an open heart that allows for greater connection and better dialogue, especially in difficult conversations. The idea here is to increase the frequency with which we function from a place of "help me understand where you are coming from."

Lastly, keep in mind some important things to know about having a difficult conversation:

- Reframe your perspective and try to find a new way of looking at it so that it simply becomes a constructive or normal conversation.
- Plan but do not script the conversation. This will allow you to identify the topics you need to talk about but also allow for the other person's perspective.
- Move from "I understand" to "help me understand."
- Listen to the other person with an open heart. Make sure the other person knows you have everyone's best interest at hand; even when you need to fire someone, remember that this might be the best thing that is happening to them (rather than feeling pity).
- Do not blame the other person but rather learn what is your role in a given situation.
- Give something back: If you are laying someone off, make sure to give them a good recommendation. If you are taking away privileges, point out how can they get them back. This allows for people to see other possibilities that might not be available for them at the moment.
- Slow down. Difficult conversations should not happen in a rush or when you are not ready for them.
- Focus on the planned topics and do not allow for distractions to take you elsewhere. If the other person starts making excuses or accusing you of something, remember not to be pulled into it.
- Be clear, direct and unemotional.

PERSPECTIVE:

Come from a place of empathy. We all know the angst that comes from difficult conversations, and, at the same time, challenge her to see the conversation from a different perspective.

PREWORK:

Start by asking her about the difficult conversation she's been putting off. When she exposes the conversation, be mindful of the following:

- What is the purpose of having the conversation? What does she hope to accomplish? What would be an ideal outcome? Watch for hidden purposes.
- What assumptions is she making about this person's intentions? She may feel intimidated, belittled, ignored, disrespected, or marginalized, but be cautious to assume this was the speaker's intention. Impact does not necessarily equal intent.
- What buttons are being pushed? Take a look at her backstory. What personal history is being triggered? She may still have the conversation, but make sure she knows going into it that some of the heightened emotional state has to do with her.

- Try to adjust the perspective to a positive one for maximum effectiveness.
- Who is the opponent? What might she be thinking about this situation? Is she aware of the problem? If so, how do you think she perceives it? What are her needs and fears? Begin to reframe the opponent as a partner.
- How has your client contributed to the problem? How has the other person?
- Once she has chosen a perspective and knows the purpose and best outcome of the conversation, roleplay with her, pretending you are the other person.

The key here is to help the client see the other person as a human being, not a tool. Then, she will be able to get in the other person's shoes and start seeing herself in a new way.

WHAT GETS IN THE WAY?:
CLIENT:

Blinders on her predicted outcome: She may say something like "I get that I should have this conversation, but I already know what the outcome is—she's not going to change." Help her understand that people will surprise you in unexpected ways and she can't change others but can invite them to change. Additionally, have her think about the other person's values: What are some things that matter to them? Find common ground with her values and proceed with the conversation from there.

Fear of confrontation: This is common. People can talk about difficult conversations but when it comes to confronting the individual, they tend to get scared and would rather say nothing than bring the issue forward.

Alleged apathy: "I could have this conversation, but I don't really care." Poke around at the apathy and see what else is there. How it is aligned with her values?

COACH:

Own agenda on how you deal with difficult conversations. Maybe you're aggressive or overly passive—be mindful of your own viewpoints. Be sure not to insinuate or vocalize your own thinking or approach and remember that she is naturally creative, resourceful and whole.

Collusion: This can be a stressful session for the client and she could turn to you to help her get out of the difficult conversation. Be sure not to collude with her and remind her of the importance of having this conversation.

HOW TO USE ILLUSTRATION / QUOTE:

After reading the Douglas Stone quote, have the client think about a time where she tried to control someone else's reaction to something that happened to them. What happened? How did it serve them? How did it serve her? What could she control? What couldn't she control?

WRAPPING UP SESSION:

In wrapping up the session, ask your client in which other areas of her life is she avoiding difficult conversations. What is the most difficult part of talking about certain things for her? Now, choose a different conversation where she can put what she learned in the session into practice.

THE
COACHES' ROADMAP
&
COACHES' GYM

THE ROAD MAP

This coaching roadmap is designed to help you create a coaching pathway that works for specific situations. Below are examples of desired archetypes that reflect both the action and the being of the client. For instance, a manager might want you to work with an employee on completing tasks, which we have personified as "The Finisher". Which sessions would best serve you in expanding this client? Use this roadmap in a way that works best for you.

THE MVP

THE PEACEMAKER

THE FINISHER

THE SEAMSTRESS

THE POET

THE EXPLORER

THE TRUTH TELLER

THE GIVER

THE STRATEGIST

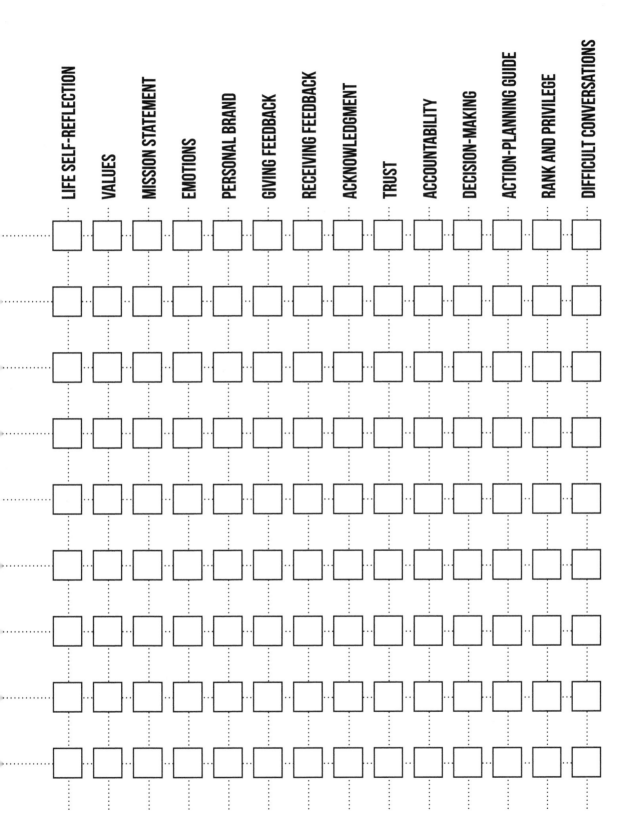

COACHES' GYM

As coaches, we understand that it's important to check in with your own state as a coach: how are we being and what are we doing? These exercises are meant to help you with your own self-development as a coach.

We go to the gym to make sure our body is fit and healthy. What exercises do we do to make sure we are functioning as the best coach we can? As with all things in life, we need a shaping, toning, and strengthening of our skills and mindsets. We hope that these exercises are useful and help you coach the best that you can.

We have separated the exercises in the three quadrants of I, WE, and IT.

After a session, sometimes a sense of dread comes to us that it did not go as planned and we hold on to it for ages, while other times we are ecstatic about a session going well but forget to gather learnings. With these simple inquiries, you will learn and make a plan forward for when things go well and when they do not. It is important to note that all of these are suggestions and you should only use the ones that feel authentic to you. We understand that with time, you will add or change things that work best for you. This is a starting point.

The being of the coach will impact the quality of the coaching session. You have to be on fire to light them on fire—you are your most important instrument, so make sure you always connect back to your purpose as a coach.

Why do you coach?

When things get rough, what do you need to remember about the work you do?

COACHES' GYM

A WARM-UP PRE-SESSIONS.

Name of client: _____. Date:_____.Session_____ of _____.

How is your body feeling?

How is your mind feeling?

How is your heart feeling?

Do any of these answers have an impact on your coaching?   YES   NO

If yes, what is your strategy to have a better impact?

Is there anything that you need to disclose to your client that you are holding back?   YES   NO

If yes, when and how would be the right way to deal with this?

Do you need to clear yourself before your client?

Do you need to connect with your wiser self?

Be honest and kind to yourself. The best coaches have a strong sense of being and truth-telling.

Anything else?

B **WHAT YOU SEE IN OTHERS EXISTS IN YOU.**

What does this mean for you in your coaching?

COACHES' GYM

WHAT YOU SEE IN OTHERS EXISTS IN YOU.

Are you attracting certain types of clients?
What do you need to know about this?

Have you listened to another way of coaching?

What is the last new thing you learned about coaching?

WHAT YOU SEE IN OTHERS EXISTS IN YOU.

Is there something you cannot be with that is
affecting your relationship with your clients?

How long ago were you coached?

COACHES' GYM

C **HUMILITY AS A COACH.**
At times, you will need to remember the importance of
humility as a coach. When you start thinking that you are
responsible for your client's elevated states of consciousness
or material gains, we want you to do the following exercise:

> *Imagine your client before she knew you. Think about being with her
> when she lost her first chemistry set, got her heart broken, or was
> accepted into her first choice school with a full scholarship. Imagine
> her in as many moments as you can before you came into her life.*

Remind yourself that her success has nothing to do with you. It
has to do with her hard work and circumstances that she has been
able to capitalize on. Now, imagine that the universe of things is a
whole year in human life, with 52 weeks and 365 days, if you think
about your contribution, how much do you think it amounts to? One
week? One day? Maybe for one hour? Reflect on your thoughts.

D OVERALL ENERGY.

After your coaching session, reflect back on the questions and overall energy of the time:

Do you tend to ask the same questions over and over again, like "How does that feel?" or "What does that look like?" or "What else?" This is an easy place to find oneself as a coach and an important one to escape. Remember to elevate the awareness, listen and speak your own intuition, be curious about the subtleties you notice.

Broaden your word bank by noticing what is happening in level 3 listening. In the space below, come up with 15 questions that would have been useful for deepening the learning for your client:

1

2

3

4

5

6

7

8

9

10

11

12

13

14

15

Did you use range by using your voice and your body? If no, what kept you from doing it?

What is the cost of not doing it?

What do you need to work on to have more range?

COACHES' GYM

(BETWEEN YOU AND YOUR COACHEE)

The session with your client starts before she calls you. It starts a few minutes before when you are connecting with who she is and where she is on her journey. The energy will be significantly different if you do a five minute connecting practice before your calls instead of going straight into your sessions.

A SET AN INTENTION FOR YOUR CLIENT.

Name of client: _____. Date:_____. Session_____ of _____.

I intend to create...

I long for this client...

What's it like setting an intention for your client?

COACHES' GYM

B THE EDGE.

What about this client is an edge for me?
Clear any assumptions.

C CLIENTS' EXPANSIVENESS.

How much coaching has your client had? While some clients' familiarity with coaching and therapy allows them to easily go to dark places or experiment with their body, other clients may be awkward or uncomfortable.

How have you designed your alliance with your client?

How comfortable is your client in using her body?

If she's fairly uncomfortable, remember that the body is an access point to a lot of information. If your client is resistant to the body, consider the following:
- Instead of saying something like "where in your body do you feel that?", try for something like "have you ever had a hunch?" or "have you ever felt nerves in your body" and go from there.
- Know your client and ask her what she is willing to do.

What are some metaphors you can offer? For instance, if the client mentions fear, say "is it like fear of a snake approaching you on a hike or fear before taking a big exam?". Neither one may resonate for them, but it at least gets her imagination working. Brainstorm some metaphors below:

1
2
3
4
5

Reflect on a relationship with a client who is more of a thinker than a feeler. Brainstorm some other ways to access the body:

1
2
3
4
5

COACHES' GYM

D **POST-SESSION REFLECTIONS.**

What did you learn from your client or from this session about yourself?

In one or two words, how would you describe your relationship with your client?

Is this what you want?   YES   NO

If no, what needs to change to create something different?

What do you need to let go of?

COACHES' GYM

A BIG PICTURE.

Take a step back and look at the broader view of your coaching sessions.

What is showing up as a pattern?

Does this pattern need to change? If yes, what needs to be different?

What percentage of coaching as opposed to consulting are you doing? How much do you want to do?

Is there a balance of focus on your clients' actions and their being? If not, what needs to change?

 **OVERALL PROCESS.**

Are your sponsors really into it?   YES   NO

If no, what is causing the distance? What needs to be
addressed that is not being said?

Looking back on your alliance, was it good or is there
something you can do differently next time?

COACHES' GYM

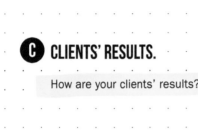 **CLIENTS' RESULTS.**

How are your clients' results?

Are they coming in above or below your expectations? Their expectations?

What is your note-taking process?

What's working and what is not?

What needs to change?

FAQ
GLOSSARY
BIBLIOGRAPHY

FAQ

HOW DO I PITCH MY COACHING BUSINESS TO A CORPORATION?

When you go into a corporation, always do your research and ask yourself:

- What is their need? (for example: high-potentials, on-boarding, first-time managers, expats, etc.)
- What can you help them alleviate? (for example: downsizing, cultural shift, transitions, low morale, communication, etc.)
- How are you going to do it? Use the coaching roadmap as your starting point. Listen to your clients' pain points and build a journey that best suits their needs.

Additionally, make sure you know the following:
- The department that is in charge of coaching. For example, sometimes it can be in HR, and other times it can be Learning and Development, or Leadership and Development, and so on. This is useful to know even when your foot in the door comes from another department; you might have met a marketing director who started with you as a client or a friend and wants you to offer your services. So, find the department in charge of coaching, otherwise, it will be an uphill battle to get them on board.
- If they have had previous coaching providers.

Be ready to co-create. Many companies are already doing some sort of coaching or mentoring, they might already use certain assessments or even have a leadership academy. Always listen to them and be flexible in creating programs that will fit them and their needs. Think about taking their leaders through a journey instead of a series of coaching sessions and consider the following: maybe you do a Life Self-Reflection exercise, or start with a workshop? Make sure you know how to sustain the learning from coaching sessions, which could be a six month checkpoint with the company and your clients.

HOW LONG SHOULD THE PROCESS TAKE?

This really depends on the company. Sometimes there are blended learning processes that include workshops, online learning, and sessions where you might only do one or two coaching sessions. Other times, there are coaching services to people when they need it and you might only get to be with a client for one session. In the corporate world, the average is between six to eight sessions.

WHAT DO I DO IF A CONFLICT OF INTEREST ARISES?

Companies usually make you sign a non-disclosure agreement ("NDA"), especially public companies that want to make sure you will not use any information shared by your coachees with anyone. The NDA goes a step further from a coaching agreement. That is, if the NDA is broken, you could end up in court, so never share if you learn that CEO is thinking about retiring, a business unit is going under, or the company is about to restructure.

WHAT DO I DO IF THE COMPANY IS A MESS - LOW EMPLOYEE SATISFACTION AND PRODUCTIVITY RATES?

- Smaller companies: When you are only hired as a coach in smaller companies, you might not be able to give much feedback to the system about themes and patterns that are not conducive to good employee satisfaction or productivity. Make sure whoever sponsored the process is given a report at the end of the intervention. Always approach this as generous feedback, one that is intended to shed light and grow them in the areas of opportunity. Inexperienced coaches might complain and point fingers at culture or other issues, making it difficult to integrate the feedback.

- Bigger companies: When you are hired as a coach for bigger companies, the data and reporting is part of your selling pitch, so be sure to include it in your confidentiality agreement with the coachee. Tell them that the company will get a report on themes and patterns that you hear among your coachees and that you will not share who said what. You create this compendium, which sometimes includes anonymous quotes (do not reveal the name or position of the person).

HOW DO I DEAL WITH A DIFFICULT CLIENT?

In the many years of coaching, Maria has only had three problem clients who she did not want to keep coaching. The reasons were insulting comments towards women, narcissistic personality, and constant lying. All of them were addressed directly to the client first and then escalated with HR. It is important to have a conversation of what a difficult client looks like and what would constitute an engagement break. She also recommends that you always have a partner coach when you come into corporations, for it will allow you to refer to this person (and the company already knows him/her).

HOW SHOULD I STRUCTURE MY FEES?

Be consistent across clients and across similar services you provide. For instance, we have seen coaches who get too greedy with big clients and charge less with smaller clients. If big clients find out about the inconsistency, it will not be good for your business. Also, be sure to charge for the design of material, meetings, and travel time separately. This might be a big number the first month of the engagement, but once it is done the cost for the companies goes down. We recommend thinking about a fee that aligns with your values, your way of working, and the income you want to make.

HOW DO I ENSURE A COMPATIBLE RELATIONSHIP?

There are two schools of thought on this topic: 1) Let the clients choose their coach after a small interview or reviewing resumes; or 2) assign coaches to clients at random. We adhere to the latter, as long as you have a strong group of coaches who have enough hours of training, we do not see "personality or compatibility" being an issue. If it is, be curious. Try getting coached by your peer to see if there is something in their style that might be getting in the way.

HOW DO I TRACK TANGIBLE PROGRESS?

Use the BDG Model for the big changes and co-create key performance indicators (KPIs) with your client:

- What part of your being do you want to improve? How will you know when you get there?
- What part of your doing (behaviors or actions) do you want to improve on? How will you know when you get there?
- What do you hope to get? How can you measure it?

HOW TO CREATE A CONTRACT?

The International Coach Federation (ICF) has a useful template to help you create your contract: https://coachfederation.org/app/uploads/2017/11/SampleCoachingAgreement.pdf.

GLOSSARY

Accountability
According to the online dictionary from Merriam-Webster, "accountability" means "an obligation or willingness to accept responsibility or to account for one's actions." It's important to remember that with accountability, there are two parties at play: The person who is assigning the task and the person who is agreeing to complete the task. Accountability is not about mandating, but rather conversing, and adjusting your message depending on what motivates the other person is vital.

Acknowledgement
The etymology of "acknowledgment" is from Middle English ancnawan, which means "recognize and understand"; the current Oxford definition is "acceptance as truth or existence of something." When we acknowledge someone, we create space for them and even in the face of conflict, when we acknowledge someone, we remind ourselves that shared humanity exists between us and that we are not alone. Unlike feedback, which is about what you do, acknowledgment is about who you are.

Attitude
Psychologists define attitudes as a "learned tendency to evaluate things in a certain way," which includes objects, ideas, events, or other people. Be cognizant that your client may have certain attitudes about certain objects or people.

Behavior
According to the online dictionary from Merriam-Webster, this is the "way in which one conducts oneself." As Eric Greitens discusses in *Resilience*, our repeated behaviors link to our identity and personal brand.

Collusion
This is the tendency for the coach to appease or agree with the client when they need truth-telling and accountability. For instance, it could look something like, "Yes, it sounds like your boss is difficult, so keep on doing what you're doing." Be mindful of this in your coaching relationship.

Commitment
Being dedicated to a cause or activity. In order for the client-coach relationship to work, both the client and the coach need to be committed to growth and connection.

Daniel Goleman's Three Types of Empathy

According to Daniel Goleman, science journalist and author of *Emotional Intelligence*, there are three types of empathy:

- Cognitive Empathy: This is "try to walk a mile in someone else's shoes"—it is the awareness and understanding of someone else's perspective which is essential for good communication and connection.
- Social Empathy: This is "sensing in yourself what another person might be feeling". For him, this is all about rapport and you can only have rapport if you "pay full attention to the other human being".
- Empathetic Concern: This is not just about feeling someone else's distress, but also wanting to help them. He goes on to say, "It draws on a third part of the brain called 'ancient mammalian system for parenting'. It's like a parent's love for a child. If you have that love for someone, you're going to be there for them."

The Domino Effect

In The ONE Thing, Gary Keller presents the idea that a domino, on its own, doesn't amount to much—it's about 2 inches in height and 9 grams in weight. But it has the ability to knock down another domino 1.5x its size. Keller goes on to ask you to imagine a long string of dominoes lined up with each one progressively 1.5x larger than the last. If you were to knock down the first two-inch domino, you would set off a chain reaction that by the 57th iteration would produce enough force to knock over a domino stretching the distance between the earth and the moon. This two-inch domino is a force and when aligned creates something much greater than itself. The same theory rings true for achievement—creating action in small increments is the path to success.

E-motions

The Coaches' Training Institute defines "e-motions" as "energy in motion." It is important to know that emotions are part of the human experience. Clients get into trouble when they suppress certain emotions whereas the resourceful clients have access to all of their emotions.

Empathy

The term "empathy" was first introduced by psychologist Edward B. Titchener in 1909 and translates as the German term *einfühlung*, meaning "feeling into." Empathy involves the ability to put yourself in someone else's position and feel what they must be feeling.

Fear

According to the online dictionary from Merriam-Webster, this is "an unpleasant emotion caused by the belief that someone or something is dangerous, likely to cause pain or a threat." As human beings, we all experience fear—the idea is to not let it run your life. Fear is like a saboteur—it may protect you from getting hurt, but will prevent you from growth and true self-expression.

Feedback

This is information about how one is doing in order to reach a goal. Unlike acknowledgment, which is about the individual, feedback is about what you do and the task at hand.

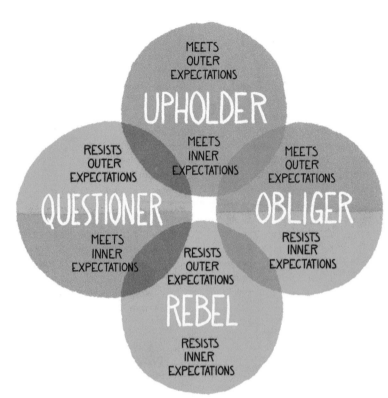

The Four Tendencies

According to Gretchen Rubin, author of The Four Tendencies, we all have inner and outer expectations. Inner expectations are those that are within us (for example, a resolution for the New Year) and outer expectations are those that are outer to us (such as meeting a work deadline or answering a friend's request). From the inner and outer expectations, each individual falls into one of four categories: Upholders, Questioners, Obligers, and Rebels. Her framework explains why we act and why we do not act.

- Upholders meet both inner and outer expectations. They do not have problems sticking to their resolutions and are the employees who meet goals (without the boss checking on them).
- Questioners meet inner expectations but resist outer expectations put upon them by others. When asked to do something, they might respond with some form of "why?"; if they receive a satisfactory answer, they may or may not follow through.
- Obligers meet outer expectations but struggle with meeting their own expectations.
- Rebels struggle with both inner and outer expectations. Rubin's slogan for them is: "You can't make me, and I can't either."

This shows how a conflict over resources (who gets what) is usually the most visible aspect of any disagreement Yet, underneath the argument is a layer of conflicting objectives. One layer deeper are the fundamental issues around identities and personal values. It is important to distinguish the layers to understand what is happening with you and the other individual so that you are able to discuss the real issues.

Goal

An aim or desired result. As Locke and Latham describe in A Theory of Goal-Setting and Task Performance, it is important for a goal to be specific, measurable, and the right level of challenge.

Iceberg Model

Jay Rothman, professor of Conflict Management at Bar-Ilan University, imagines conflict as something like the iceberg model below:

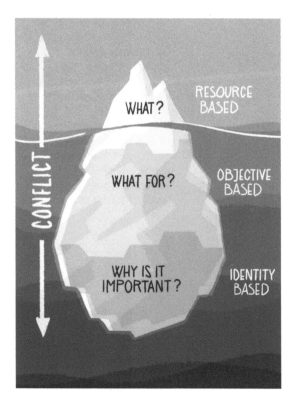

Ken Wilber's Four Quadrants

- **Quadrant 1**, or **I**, is the individual and subjective aspect of the change. It is the inner reality of people. It is the area of cognitive, psychological, and spiritual development. In this quadrant, leaders attend to the internal development of people, recognizing that a substantive change without a change in consciousness is not possible.

- **Quadrant 2**, or **WE**, is related to the individual and objective aspect of the change. This is the terrain of technical skills and observable behavior and takes much of the attention from coaches and great athletes. It is where leaders pay attention to the development of people's skills and support the physical and psychological ingredients that activate motivation and high performance.

- **Quadrant 3**, or **IT**, addresses the group and subjective aspects of change. It is the land of culture. It is the inner territory, often hidden, of the shared assumptions and imagery that direct what happens when the team or group meets. It is the domain of myth, history, unwritten rules, and/or beliefs. This quadrant reminds leaders to pay attention to the deeper meanings of symbols, purpose, vision, and values; deeper meanings not so much in their written form but in the subtle messages encoded in daily interactions.

- **Quadrant 4**, or **ITS**, has to do with the group and objective aspects of the change, the social, technical, and organizational system. It is the quadrant of organizational design, flow technology, policies, and procedures. This quadrant reminds leaders that system design determines performance, and if we want to elevate performance, we must design it accordingly.

Life Self-Reflection

An exercise that integrates the past, the present, and the future. It not only includes what we did but also how we did it—and what was happening that prevented us or supported us in our endeavor. It also helps us to take time to visualize what we want to leave behind or bring with us, as we move from the present to the future.

Limiting Beliefs

Beliefs that constrain us— about ourselves, our identity, other people, or the world in general. They are usually derived from our experience, upbringing, education, or fears.

Method in Decision-Making

Method is the process by which decisions are made. According to Patterson, Grenny, McMillan, and Switzler, there are four methods of decision-making:

- Command – Decisions are made externally either because we do not care enough to be involved or because we fully trust the decision maker.
- Consult – Decision makers invite others to influence them before making their choice. This consists of gathering ideas, evaluating options, making a choice, and informing others.
- Vote - This is self-explanatory. It is best where efficiency is the highest value and you are selecting from several good choices. It only works when all team members feel that they can support either choice.
- Consensus – Decisions are made after everyone honestly agrees on one decision. Only use this when: 1) the stakes are high and issues are complex; 2) issues where everyone absolutely must support the final choice.

Mission Statement

A mission statement is a simple tool that encapsulates what they stand for and how they want to create impact. It is something to use when difficult decisions arise and they need to know if it will take them closer or further from the path they have set for themselves and others.

The ONE Thing

In his book, The ONE Thing, Gary Keller shows that every successful person has identified their ONE Thing. Their ONE Thing is what they want in the long-run. It is specific to them and because they have spotted it, they are able to dismiss distractions and concentrate on their ONE Thing.

Perspective

According to the online dictionary from Merriam-Webster, "perspective" is a point of view or "a particular way of looking a something." As a coach, it's important to hold a perspective that allows for the growth of your client.

Personal Brand

Personal brand is the collection of our perceptions, behaviors, feelings, and responses to anything that happens to us. To create personal brand, it's crucial to be aware of the following: present context, feelings about the current position, perception of the world/job/situation, how we want to respond/impact it, and behavior.

Privilege

Privilege is a right given only to some, and not all. Some privileges are granted based on merit, like gaining entry to a school's alumni body. Others are based on unearned factors such as ethnicity or gender.

Rank

Rank is an accumulation of power and privilege that is situational and changes over time. According to Arnold Mindell, an American author, therapist, and teacher, there are three types of rank:

- Social rank is almost always unearned based on nationality, family, gender, ethnicity.
- Situational rank is situational and individual specific. What might provide a rank in a certain space, like being a priest in your church, might not grant rank in another space where your title does not grant you power or privilege.
- Psychological rank is gained by the challenges that we overcome over a lifetime of experiences. A person who has high psychological rank will be more likely to become a leader in an organization because it will show in the way they speak, act and make decisions.

Reflective Cycle

In *Learning by Doing: a Guide to Teaching and Learning Methods*, Gibbs Graham developed a cycle to be used in a learning situation. Today, it is often used by the healthcare industry but is also a great tool to integrate feedback in an organized manner in which we are not clouded by emotions. Graham's reflective cycle is a process involving six steps:

- Description - What happened?
- Feelings - What did you think and feel about it?
- Evaluation - What were the positives and negatives?
- Analysis - What sense can you make of it? If only 2% were true, what would that be?
- Conclusion - What else could you have done?
- Action Plan - What will you do next time?

It is a cycle because the action you take in the final stage will feed back into the first stage, beginning the process again.

Roleplay

This may appear in the client-coach relationship. It is when an individual acts out a role—a part, a particular person, or a character—in accordance with how she is perceived by society. The idea is to create a situation in which the client can experience how she would like to act.

Saboteur

The voice that comes in different shades and sizes, from the "I do not have time," or "I am too old for that," to the "I do not deserve it and they do not want me." It tries to keep us away from living in flow and informs us of possible scenarios in which we might get hurt or disappointed. They keep us in our safe place and prevent us from growth.

Self-Awareness

Daniel Goleman defines this as "knowing one's internal states, preferences, resources, and intuitions." It's important to know that self-awareness is not only what we notice about ourselves, but also how we observe our inner world. Self-awareness comes with no judgment and with an open heart and mind.

Eight Pillars of Trust

David Horsager, author of The Trust Edge: How Top Leaders Gain Faster Results, Deeper Relationships, and a Stronger Bottom Line argues that everything of value is built on trust, as it has always been foundational to genuine success, be it relationships or financial institutions. In his studies, he found that the top organizations and leaders have a competitive advantage over others in that they are able to weather storms and maintain respect with customers; that competitive advantage is that they are the most trusted. With this, he has been able to dissect the components of what we know through that trust. To him, there are eight pillars of trust:

- Clarity: People trust the clear and mistrust or distrust the ambiguous.
- Compassion: People put faith in those who care beyond themselves.
- Character: People notice those who do what is right ahead of what is easy.
- Contribution: Few things build trust quicker than actual results.
- Competency: People have confidence in those who stay fresh, relevant, and capable.
- Connection: People want to follow, buy from, and be around friends—and having friends is all about building connections.
- Commitment: People believe in those who stand through adversity.
- Consistency: In every area of life, it's the little things—done consistently—that make the big difference.

Strategies in Decision-Making

According to Dr. Joel Hoomans, there are six decision strategies:

- **Impulsiveness** – Leverage the first option you are given and be done with it.
- **Compliance** – Go with the most pleasing and popular option as it pertains to those impacted.
- **Delegating** – Push decisions off to capable and trusted others.
- **Avoidance/Deflection** – Ignore as many decisions as possible in an effort to avoid responsibility for their impact or just prevent them from overwhelming you.
- **Balancing** – Weigh the factors involved and then use them to render the best decision in the moment.
- **Prioritizing & Reflecting** – Put the most energy, thought and effort into those decisions that will have the greatest impact. Maximize the time you have in which to make those decisions by consulting with others, considering the context, etc.

Trust

Trust sets the foundation for strong relationships. It is mutual confidence and safety felt in one another. It's important to create a baseline of what you need so that you can trust others and see how you might be measuring up to your own standards.

Values

According to the Oxford English Dictionary, "value" is "one's judgment about what is important in life." Thus, values are who you are in your life today, not who you want to be or who others (or you) think you should be. They define what is most important to us and form the basis for what we will and will not do.

BIBLIOGRAPHY

"Anatomy of Trust." Smalley Institute, 24 Jan. 2019, https://www.smalleyinstitute.com/blog/anatomy-of-trust. Accessed 27 Mar. 2019.

Arruda, William. Ditch, Dare, Do: 3D Personal Branding for Executives. Trades-Marke Press, 2013.

Boud, David. Reflection: Turning Experience into Learning, RoutledgeFalmer, Oxon, 1985.

"Build Your Capacity. Enhance Your Impact." LeaderShift, https://www.leadershiftproject.ca/uploads/1/1/8/4/118409684/providing_feedback_leadershift_webinar_deck.pdf. Accessed 1 Apr. 2019.

Camp, Jim. "Decisions Are Largely Emotional, Not Logical: The Neuroscience Behind Decision-Making." Big Think. 11 Jun. 2012, https://bigthink.com/experts-corner/decisions-are-emotional-not-logical-the-neuroscience-behind-decision-making. Accessed 27 Mar. 2019.

Cherry, Kendra. "Attitudes and Behavior in Psychology." VeryWellMind, 20 Sep. 2018, https://www.verywellmind.com/attitudes-how-they-form-change-shape-behavior-2795897. Accessed 27 Mar. 2019.

Frankel, Viktor E. Man's Search for Meaning. Beacon Press, 2006.

Glaze, JE. "Reflection as a Transforming Process: Students

Advanced Nurse Practitioners' Experiences of Developing Reflective Skills as Part of an MSc Programme." Journal of Advanced Nursing 34.5 (2001): 639-647. 27 Mar. 2019.

Goleman, Daniel. Emotional Intelligence. Bantam Books, 1995.

Graham, Gibbs. Learning by Doing: a Guide to Teaching and Learning Methods. Oxford, 1988.

Greiner, Rae. "1909: The Introduction of the Word 'Empathy' into English." Branch, 2019, http://www.branchcollective.org/?ps_articles=rae-greiner-1909-the-introduction-of-the-word-empathy-into-english. Accessed 27 Mar. 2019.

Greitens, Eric. Resilience: Hard-Won Wisdom for Living a Better Life. Houghton Mifflin Harcourt, 2015.

Hoomans, Joel, "35,000 Decisions: The Great Choices of Strategic Leaders." Roberts Wesleyan College, 20 Mar. 2015, https://go.roberts.edu/leadingedge/the-great-choices-of-strategic-leaders. Accessed 27 Mar. 2019.

Horsager, David. The Trust Edge: How Top Leaders Gain Faster Results, Deeper Relationships, and a Stronger Bottom Line. Free Press, 2009.

Keller, Gary. The ONE Thing: The Surprisingly Simple Truth Behind Extraordinary Results. Bard Press, 2013.

Kindschi, Douglas. "Coming from Earth: Humus, Humanity, Humility." Grand Rapids Press, 14 Sep 2017, https://www.gvsu.edu/cms4/asset/843249C9-B1E5-BD47-A25EDBC68363B726/grandrapidspress_2017-sep_14_from_the_earth_-_humus_humanity_humility.pdf. Accessed 27 Mar. 2019.

Kornfield, Jack. "Identity and Selflessness in Buddhism: No Self or True Self?" tricycle, 2019, https://tricycle.org/magazine/no-self-or-true-self/. Accessed 27 Mar. 2019.

Kraemer, Harry M. From Values to Action: The Four Principles of Value-Based Leadership, Wiley, 2011.

Lenzen, Manuela. "Feeling Our Emotions." Scientific Journal. 2019, https://www.scientificamerican.com/article/feeling-our-emotions/. Accessed 27 Mar. 2019.

Locke, Edwin A., and Gary P Latham. "Theory of Goal-Setting and Task Performance." The Academy of Management Review 16.2 (1991): 480-483. 27 Mar. 2019.

Matua, Gerald A., Vidya Seshan, Adenike A. Akintola, Anitha N. Thanka. "Strategies for Providing Effective Feedback During Preceptorship: Perspectives from an Omani Hospital." Journal of Nursing Education and Practice 4.10 (2014): 24-31. 27 Mar. 2019.

Merriam-Webster.com. Merriam-Webster, 2019.

Mindell, Arnold. Sitting in the Fire: Large Group Transformation Using Conflict and Diversity. Deep Democracy Exchange, 1995.

Moyle, Sally. "Giving Feedback - 3 Models for Effective Feedback." Ausmed, 15 Feb. 2017, https://www.ausmed.com/cpd/articles/giving-feedback. Accessed 27 Mar. 2019.

OxfordDictionaries.com. Oxford Dictionaries, 2019.

Patterson, Kerry. Crucial Conversations: Tools for Talking When Stakes are High. McGraw-Hill, 2012.

Perel, Esther. "The communication error we all make, and how it intensifies conflict." Big Think. 24 Mar. 2018, https://bigthink.com/videos/esther-perel-the-communication-error-we-all-make-and-how-it-intensifies-conflict. Accessed 24 Oct. 2019.

Piandes, Adam. "How to Be Efficient With Your Personal Acknowledgement." Forbes, 3 May 2017, https://www.forbes.com/sites/forbescoachescouncil/2017/05/03/how-to-be-efficient-with-your-personal-acknowledgement/#5c71c1c97d61. Accessed 27 Mar. 2019.

Rose, Miranda and Dawn Best. Transforming Practice Through Clinical Education, Professional Supervision and Mentoring. Churchill Livingston, 2005.

Rothman, Jay, "Conflict Engagement: A Contingency Model in Theory and Practice." NSUWorks 21.2 (2014). 27 Mar 2019.

Rubin, Gretchen. The Four Tendencies: The Indispensable Personality Profiles That Reveal How to Make Your Life Better (and Other People's Lives Better, Too). Harmony Books, 2017.

Schon, Donald. The Reflective Practitioner: How Professionals Think in Action, Basic Books, 1983.

Strozzi-Heckler, Richard. The Leadership Dojo: Build Your Foundation as an Exemplary Leader. Frog Books, 2011.

"Study Focuses on Strategies for Achieving Goals, Resolutions." Dominican University of California, 2019 https://www.dominican.edu/dominicannews/study-highlights-strategies-for-achieving-goals. Accessed 27 Mar. 2019.

"Tools - Emotional Feeling Vocabulary." The Coaches Training Institute, 2012, https://coactive.com/learning-hub/intermediate/process/res/Tools/PRO-Emotional-Field-Feeling-Vocabulary.pdf. Accessed 27 Mar. 2019.

"Use the Domino Effect to Crush Your Biggest Goal." The 1 Thing, 2019, https://www.the1thing.com/blog/the-one-thing/use-the-domino-effect-to-crush-your-biggest-goal. Accessed 3 Apr. 2019.

Valcour, Monique. "How to Give Tough Feedback That Helps People Grow." HBR, 11 Aug. 2015, https://hbr.org/2015/08/how-to-give-tough-feedback-that-helps-people-grow. Accessed 27 Mar. 2019.

Wallen, Ruth. "The Power of Acknowledgement." Goddard College, 5 May 2015, https://www.goddard.edu/2015/05/the-power-of-acknowledgement/. Accessed 27 Mar. 2019.

Wilber, Ken. "What Are the Four Quadrants?" Integral Life, 2014 Oct. 28, https://integrallife.com/four-quadrants/. Accessed 1 Apr. 2019.

Windust, Jon. "The Science of Feedback: What is the Right Frequency for Workplace Feedback?" Cognology, 26 May 2015, https://www.cognology.com.au/the-science-of-feedback-what-is-the-right-frequency-for-workplace-feedback/. Accessed 27 Mar. 2019.

ACKNOWLEDGMENTS

We want to thank our partners, Jody and Tommy, children, Milo and Olivia, family, and friends for all their support and belief in us throughout this journey. We would also like to thank Ana Luisa Ugalde for the role she had in the beginning stages of the book.